THIS OLD QUILT

A Heartwarming Celebration of Quilts and Quilting Memories

Margret Aldrich, Editor

With writings, artwork, and photographs from Whitney Otto, Alice Walker, Sandra Dallas, Terry McMillan, Jennifer Chiaverini, Reba McEntire, Laura Ingalls Wilder, Harriet Beecher Stowe, Dorothy Canfield Fisher, Eliza Calvert Hall, Ami Simms, Patricia J. Cooper and Norma Bradley Allen, Bob Artley, Sandi Wickersham, and more.

■ ■ ■

VOYAGEUR PRESS

Edited by Margret Aldrich
Designed by Maria Friedrich
Printed in China

First Hardcover Edition
03 04 05 06 5 4

First Softcover Edition
05 06 07 08 09 5 4 3 2 1

Library of Congress Cataloging-in-Publication Data

Aldrich, Margret, 1975–
    This old quilt : a heartwarming celebration of quilts and quilting memories / Margret Aldrich.
        p. cm.
    First Hardcover Edition ISBN 0-89658-551-4
    First Softcover Edition ISBN 0-89658-748-7 (pbk)
    1. Quiltmakers—Fiction. 2. Quilting—Fiction. 3. Quilts—Fiction. 4. Quiltmakers. 5. Quilting. 6. Quilts. I. Title.

PS3601.L35 T48 2001
813'.6—dc21

2001026534

Distributed in Canada by Raincoast Books,
9050 Shaughnessy Street, Vancouver, B.C. V6P 6E5

Published by Voyageur Press, Inc.
123 North Second Street, P.O. Box 338,
Stillwater, MN 55082 U.S.A.
651-430-2210, fax 651-430-2211
books@voyageurpress.com
www.voyageurpress.com

Educators, fundraisers, premium and gift buyers, publicists, and marketing managers: Looking for creative products and new sales ideas? Voyageur Press books are available at special discounts when purchased in quantities, and special editions can be created to your specifications. For details contact the marketing department at 800-888-9653.

Permissions
    "How to Make an American Quilt" from *How to Make an American Quilt* by Whitney Otto. Copyright © 1991 by Whitney Otto. Used by permission of Villard Books, a division of Random House, Inc.
    "How <u>Not</u> to Make a Prize-Winning Quilt" from *How <u>Not</u> to Make a Prize-Winning Quilt* by Ami Simms. Copyright © 1994 by Ami Simms. Used by permission of the author and Mallery Press.
    "The Quilter's Apprentice" reprinted with the permission of Simon & Schuster from *The Quilter's Apprentice* by Jennifer Chiaverini. Copyright © 1999 by Jennifer Chiaverini.
    "Quilts among the Plain People" from *Quilts Among the Plain People* by Rachel T. Pellman and Joanne Ranck. Copyright © 1981 by Good Books. Used by permission of Good Books.

    "Hidden in Plain View" from *Hidden in Plain View* by Jacqueline Tobin and Raymond Dobard. Copyright © 1998 by Jacqueline Tobin and Raymond Dobard. Used by permission of Doubleday, a division of Random House, Inc.
    "Quilts and the Hopi Baby-Naming Ceremony" by Marlene Sekaquaptewa and Caroly O'Bagy Davis from *To Honor and Comfort: Native Quilting Traditions* by Marsha L. MacDowell and Kurt Dewhurst. Copyright © 1997 Museum of New Mexico Press and Michigan State University Museum. Used by permission of the Museum of New Mexico Press.
    "The Bedquilt" from *Hillsboro People* by Dorothy Canfield Fisher. Copyright © 1927 by Dorothy Canfield Fisher. Used by permission of Vivian Scott Hixson.
    "Quilting on the Rebound" by Terry McMillan. Copyright © 1991 by Terry McMillan. Used by permission of the author.
    "The Persian Pickle Club" from *The Persian Pickle Club* by Sandra Dallas. Copyright © 1995 by Sandra Dallas. Reprinted by permission of St. Martin's Press, LLC.
    "Everyday Use" from *In Love & Trouble: Stories of Black Women* by Alice Walker. Copyright © 1973 by Alice Walker. Reprinted by permission of Harcourt, Inc.
    "Comfort from a Country Quilt" from *Comfort From a Country Quilt* by Reba McEntire. Copyright © 1999 by Reba McEntire. Used by permission of Bantam Books, a division of Random House, Inc.
    "The Quilters" from *The Quilters: Women and Domestic Art: An Oral History* by Patricia J. Cooper and Norma Bradley Allen, TTU Press. Copyright © 1999 Patricia J. Cooper and Norma Bradley Allen. Used by permission of Norma Bradley Allen and Willa Baker.

Cartoons from *Cartoons: From the Newspaper Series "Memories of a Former Kid"* by Bob Artley. Copyright © 1981 by Bob Artley. Used by permission of the author.
Cartoons from *Cartoons II: From the Newspaper Series "Memories of a Former Kid"* by Bob Artley. Copyright © 1989 by Bob Artley. Used by permission of the author.

ON THE FRONTISPIECE: *This bold Broken Star quilt from the collection of Kitty Clark Cole was made circa 1890. (Photograph © Keith Baum/BaumsAway!)*

ON THE TITLE PAGES: *A quilting demonstration and quilt sale are the highlights of this small-town gathering in folk artist Sandi Wickersham's painting, "Long Awaited Country Fair." (Artwork © Sandi Wickersham)*

INSET ON THE TITLE PAGE: *A woman poses with her State quilt in Pie Town, New Mexico, in this 1940 photograph. (Library of Congress)*

ON THE FACING PAGE: WINDMILL BLADES
The many multicolored pieces of cotton, wool, and velvet in this 1850s Log Cabin variation seem to spin in constant movement. (Minnesota Historical Society)

ON THE CONTENTS PAGE: VICTORIAN CRAZY QUILT
Luxurious silk and velvet "Crazies" were the most popular type of show quilt in their heyday, which dated from the mid 1870s to the dawn of the twentieth century. (Photograph © Leslie M. Newman)

Acknowledgments

Many people have helped put this book together. My sincere thanks go to those who have shared their vision of the quilt through words and images: J. C. Allen and Son, Bob Artley, Keith Baum, Norma Bradley Allen, Paul Cirone, Molly Friedrich, and Terry McMillan, Sandra Dallas, Kent and Donna Dannen, Danny Dempster, Adele Earnshaw and Mary Marshall at Hadley Licensing, Sheila Lee Elstad, Jerry Irwin, Jerry and Barbara Jividen, Doug Knutson and Tom Benda at Apple Creek Publishing, Dianne Dietrich Leis, Leslie M. Newman, Tomy O'Brien, Bob Pettes, Diane Phalen, Tom Sierak, Ami Simms, Connie Toops, and Sandi Wickersham.

Thanks also to Jim Bowman at the Glenbow Archives, John R. Hallberg at the Institute for Regional Studies at North Dakota State University, Candy Hart at the Minnesota Historical Society, Brent Peterson at the Washington County Historical Society, Mary Wachs at the Museum of New Mexico Press, and Pearl Wong at the Michigan State University Museum.

Finally, heartfelt thanks to Gary Kunkel for his unending support, Maria Friedrich for her energy and creativity, Michael Dregni for his guidance on the project, and friends at Voyageur Press and elsewhere who offered advice or shared their own quilting stories.

Contents

This Old Quilt

■ ■ ■

The quilt has become a symbol of North American resourcefulness, ingenuity, and creativity. From scraps of cloth, a needle, thread, and thimble, and hours upon hours of painstaking precision and care, countless patchwork quilts have been born from the imaginations of a continent of quilters.

Quilting itself was not originated in North America, however; it is an ancient technique, traced to early civilizations in Asia and India. Sixteenth-century England is the birthplace of the quilt as we know it, where luxurious whole-cloth and appliquéd quilts were the height of popularity. As early colonists migrated to the New World, they brought with them the basic principles of quilting, which consisted of the simple formula of three layers (top, batting, and backing) being stitched together to form a thick, warm bedcover. Because fabric was scarce in Colonial days, sensible women began "piecing" their quilt tops with scraps of leftover cloth from other sewing projects. By the early nineteenth century, these pieced quilts had evolved into the "block" form that is celebrated today as the quintessential North American quilting style.

Hundreds of quilt blocks and patterns have been imagined over the decades, from the Bear's Paw to the Bow Tie, the Endless Chain to the Evening Star, and the Honeycomb to the Hands of Friendship. The innumerable variations of quilt blocks and block arrangements allowed the quilter unending combinations and possibilities. This domestic art form was soon adopted by local cultures who modified the patchwork quilt to incorporate their own beliefs and experiences. Amish quiltmakers used the richly colored fabric of their clothing to make distinctively strong, simple designs; African American quilters often fused bold African designs with traditional quilt patterns; and Native American quilters frequently included important tribal symbols in their quilts. The complexities of the quilt allowed women of all backgrounds to become the creators of something original, beautiful, highly personal, and strongly self-identified.

"A STITCH IN TIME"
Massachusetts-based artist Tom Sierak captures a granddaughter's first quilting lesson in this reproduction of his original heartwarming pastel painting. (Artwork © Tom Sierak)

Quilting also brought women together, as networks were formed by the women who regularly met to swap a new quilt block design or a tried-and-true method for achieving the perfect quilting stitch. Often, quilting bees were organized for a philanthropic purpose: Quilts were made to give away to departing friends, future brides, town ministers, or the less fortunate. The slow, steady work of quilting provided the women time to talk. Uninterrupted by a pot that needed to be washed or a floor that needed to be swept, they were able to share heartfelt cares and concerns with their fellow quiltmakers. These quilting circles produced mountains of quilts as well as fast friendships.

Today, a multitude of women carry on the quilting tradition. In a recent survey, it was estimated that there are twenty million quilters in the United States alone. Perhaps they are the next generation of a long line of quilters, or perhaps they are the first in their family to thread a needle; perhaps they remember sitting by their grandmother's side as she pieced a many-colored quilt, or perhaps their first contact with patchwork was through a quilt-shop window. Whatever their backgrounds, quilters are able to write their own life experiences and histories into the yielding text of the fabric. A diary of the joys and sorrows of a lifetime are stitched into the quilt, and as it will be passed from the quiltmaker to future generations, it serves as a promise that she will not be forgotten.

The pieces collected in this anthology make up a patchwork of quilting experience. There are contemporary works of fiction from authors Terry McMillan, Whitney Otto, Sandra Dallas, Jennifer Chiaverini, and Alice Walker; classic stories from Eliza Calvert Hall, Mary Eleanor Wilkins Freeman, and Dorothy Canfield Fisher; humorous words of instruction from quilter Ami Simms; fascinating facts and lore from quilt historians Jacqueline L. Tobin and Raymond G. Dobard, Rachel T. Pellman and Joanne Ranck, and Marlene Sekaquaptewa and Carolyn O'Bagy Davis; and a scrapbook of quilting memories, recorded by Patricia J. Cooper and Norma Bradley Allen.

The photographs come from a range of respected photographers and archives, including Keith Baum, Daniel Dempster, Jerry Irwin, J. C. Allen

From yesterday to you

Patchwork is a wonderful way to pass memories from one generation to the next. Special quilts, like this turn-of-the-century Mennonite Postage Stamp quilt from the collection of Kitty Clark Cole, were often given as gifts to celebrate happy occasions. (Photograph © Keith Baum/BaumsAway!)

and Son, Jerry and Barbara Jividen, Connie Toops, Dianne Dietrich Leis, Kent and Donna Dannen, and Leslie M. Newman.

In addition, there are beautiful paintings from Sandi Wickersham, Bob Pettes, Adele Earnshaw, Tom Sierak, Diane Phalen, Sheila Lee Elstad, and Doug Knutson, as well as a selection of drawings from well-loved rural observer Bob Artley, best known for his syndicated *Memories of a Former Kid* series.

This book is a kaleidoscope of colorful bits and pieces, joined together in the tradition of the glorious patchwork quilt it celebrates.

WHAT'S IN A NAME?
Naming a new quilt block took careful consideration. Some patterns, like Democrat Rose and Lincoln's Platform, had a political theme; others, like Carpenter's Wheel and Churn Dash came from the labors of everyday life. This 1860s Sunburst quilt, with a vine and berry border, takes its name and its inspiration from the natural world. (Minnesota Historical Society)

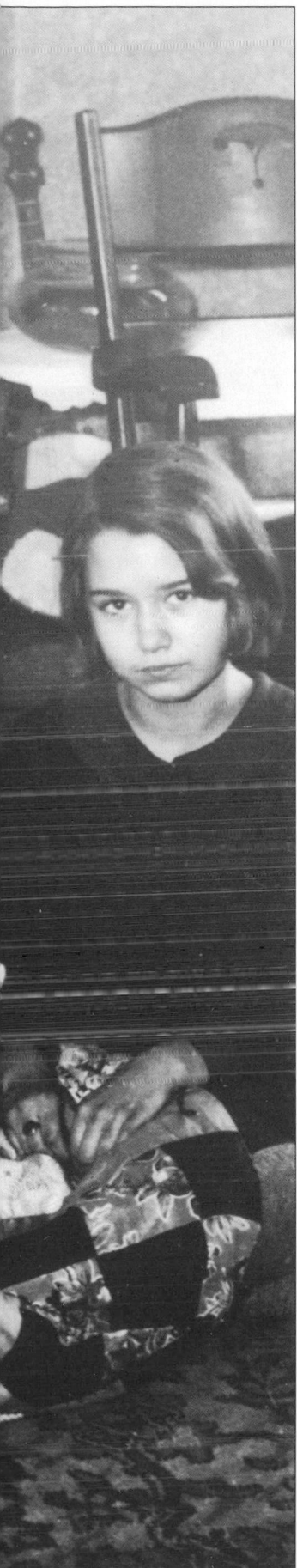

CHAPTER I

The First Stitch

"Patchwork? Ah, no! It was memory, imagination, history, biography, joy, sorrow, philosophy, religion, romance, realism, life, love, and death; and over all, like a halo, the love of the artist for his work and the soul's longing for earthly immortality."
—Eliza Calvert Hall, Aunt Jane of Kentucky, 1898

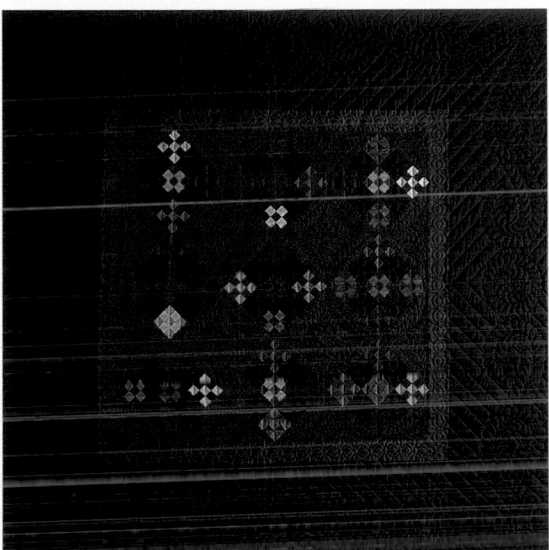

*E*very quilter must start as a beginner. The mysteries of how to keep your stitches even, your quilt blocks smooth, and your binding straight are hard-learned lessons, and students often pay their dues with pricked fingers and sore shoulders. Good students are open to the pieces of instruction, advice, and wisdom that flow freely from one generation of quilters to the next. The words of a willing teacher are priceless, and through them, young quilters come to realize that a quilt is made of more than just common thread and cloth—a lifetime of stories and memories are woven into the quilt just as tightly as the stitches.

The selections in this chapter celebrate the spirit of fledgling quilters everywhere.

DOUBLE NINE PATCH
ABOVE: *The Nine Patch is typically the easiest pattern to piece and quilt, as it is simply nine small squares stitched together to make one larger square. This quilt from Lovina's Stitchery in Strasburg, Pennsylvania, shows, however, that the Nine Patch can become much more complex. (Photograph © Keith Baum/BaumsAway!)*

TYING A QUILT WITH TEAMWORK
LEFT: *Ten hands are better than two in this 1935 photograph that proves you're never too young to learn how to quilt. (Photograph by George Luxton, Minnesota Historical Society)*

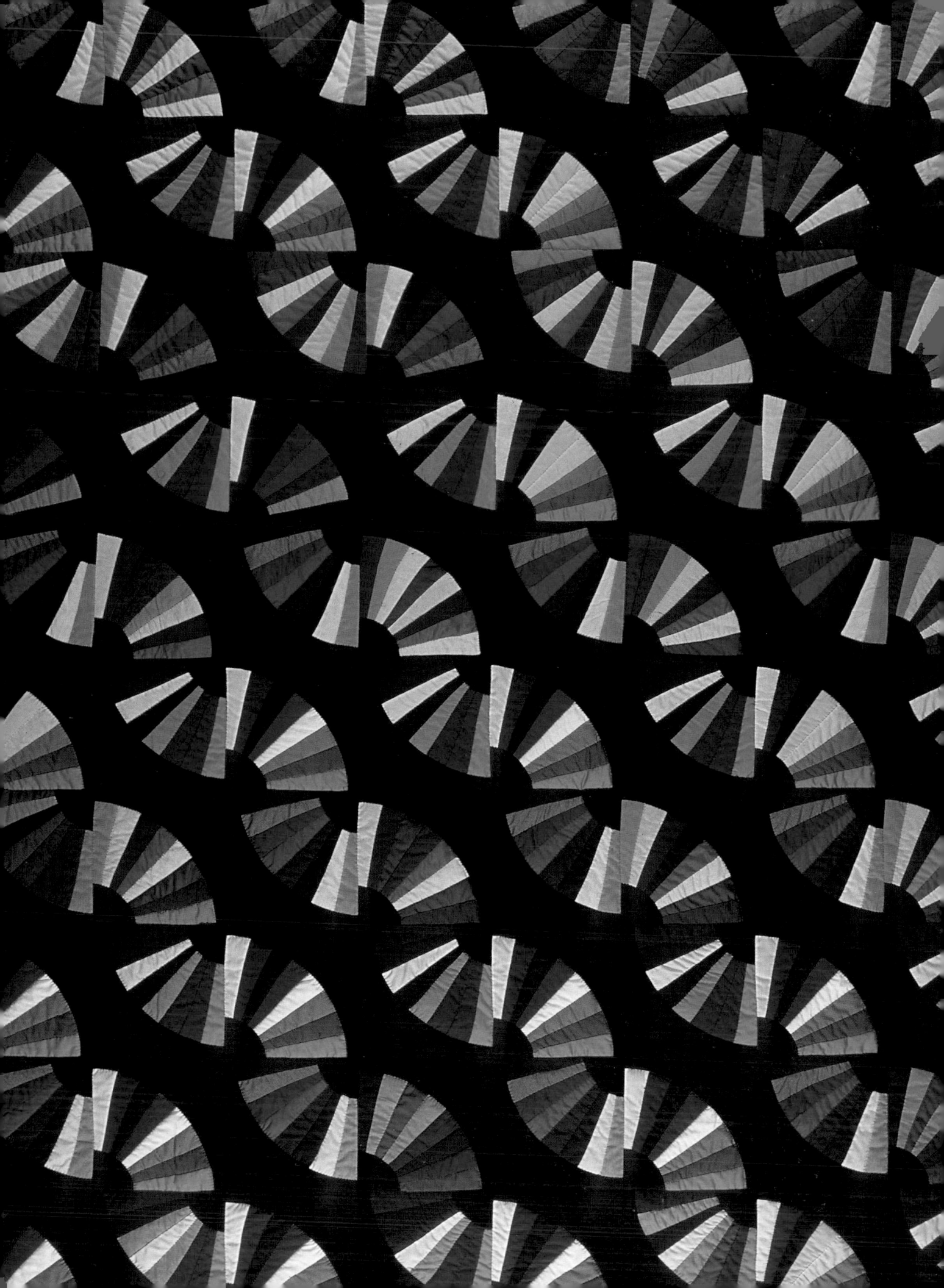

How to Make an American Quilt

By Whitney Otto

PERHAPS THE MOST important trait of an inexperienced quilter is the willingness to listen. In Whitney Otto's intriguing first novel, *How to Make an American Quilt*, a young woman named Finn decides to spend the summer in Grasse, California, with her grandmother, great aunt, and the circle of quilters that meet in their house each week. The women, varied in ages and backgrounds, come together to sew and share stories, adding steadily to the crazy quilt that they are piecing. Through the conversations of these women, Finn learns the ingredients that are necessary in making a good quilt: attention to history, expression of art, recollection of life experience—and maybe most vital, comfortable chairs and a cool pitcher of lemonade.

How to Make an American Quilt was well received by quilters and non-quilters alike. In 1995, it was made into a motion picture of the same name starring Winona Ryder and Anne Bancroft.

■ ■ ■

At first, I thought I would study art. Art history, to be exact. Then I thought, No, what about physical anthropology? a point in my life thereafter referred to as My Jane Goodall Period. I tried to imagine my mother, Sarah Bennett-Dodd (called Sally by everyone with the exception of her mother), camping with me in the African bush, drinking strong coffee from our battered tin cups, much in the way that Jane did with Mrs. Goodall. I saw us laid up with matching cases of malaria; in mother/daughter safari shorts; our hands weathering in exactly the same fashion.

Then, of course, I remembered that I was talking about *my* mother, Sally, who is most comfortable with modernity and refuses to live in a house that anyone has lived in before, exposing me to a life of tract housing that was curious and awful.

Literature was my next love. Until I became loosely acquainted with critical theory, which struck me as a kind of intellectualism for its own sake. It always seems that one has to choose literature or critical theory, that one cannot love both. All of this finally pushed me willingly (I later realized) into history.

I began with the discipline of the time line—a holdover from elementary school—setting all the dates in order, allowing me to fix time and place. History needs a specific context, if nothing else. My time lines gradually grew more and more ornate, with pasted-on photographs and drawings that I carefully cut from cheap history books possessing great illustrations but terrible, unchallenging text. I was taken with the look of

GRANDMOTHER'S FAN
This quilt from Sylvia Petersheim Quilts & Crafts in Bird-in-Hand, Pennsylvania, appears to be aflutter as fans of many colors cascade across it. (Photograph © Keith Baum/BaumsAway!)

history before I arrived at the "meat" of the matter. But the construction of the time line is both horizontal and vertical, both distance and depth. Which, finally, makes it rather unwieldy on paper. What I am saying is that it needed other dimensions, that history is not a matter of dates, and only disreputable or unimaginative teachers take the "impartial" date approach, thereby killing all interest in the subject at a very early age for many students.

(I knew, in a perfect world, I would not be forced to choose a single course of study, that I would have time for all these interests. I could gather up all my desires and count them out like valentines.)

The Victorians caught my eye almost instantly with their strange and sometimes ugly ideas about architecture and dress and social conventions. Some of it was pure whimsy, like a diorama in which ninety-two squirrels were stuffed and mounted, enacting a basement beer-and-poker party, complete with cigars and green visors pulled low over their bright eyes; or a house that displayed a painting of cherubs, clad in strips of white linen, flying above the clouds with an identical painting hidden, right next to it, under a curtain in which the same cherubs—babies though they were—are completely nude. Or a privileged Texas belle's curio cabinet that contained a human skull and blackened hand. Or still another young woman (wealthy daughter of a prominent man) who insisted on gliding through the family mansion with a handful of live kittens clinging to the train of her dress.

I enrolled in graduate school. Then I lost interest. I cared and then I didn't care. I wanted to know as much about the small, odd details that I discovered here and there when looking into the past as I did about Lenin's secret train

or England's Victorian imperialism or a flawless neo-Marxist critique of capitalism.

There were things that struck me as funny, like the name Bushrod Washington, which belonged to George's nephew, or the man who painted Mary Freake and her baby, known only as the Freake Limner. And I like that sort of historical gossip; I mean, is it true that Catherine the Great died trying to copulate with a horse? And if not, what a strange thing to say about someone. Did Thomas Jefferson have a lengthy, fruitful affair with his slave Sally Hemings? What does that say about the man who was the architect of the great

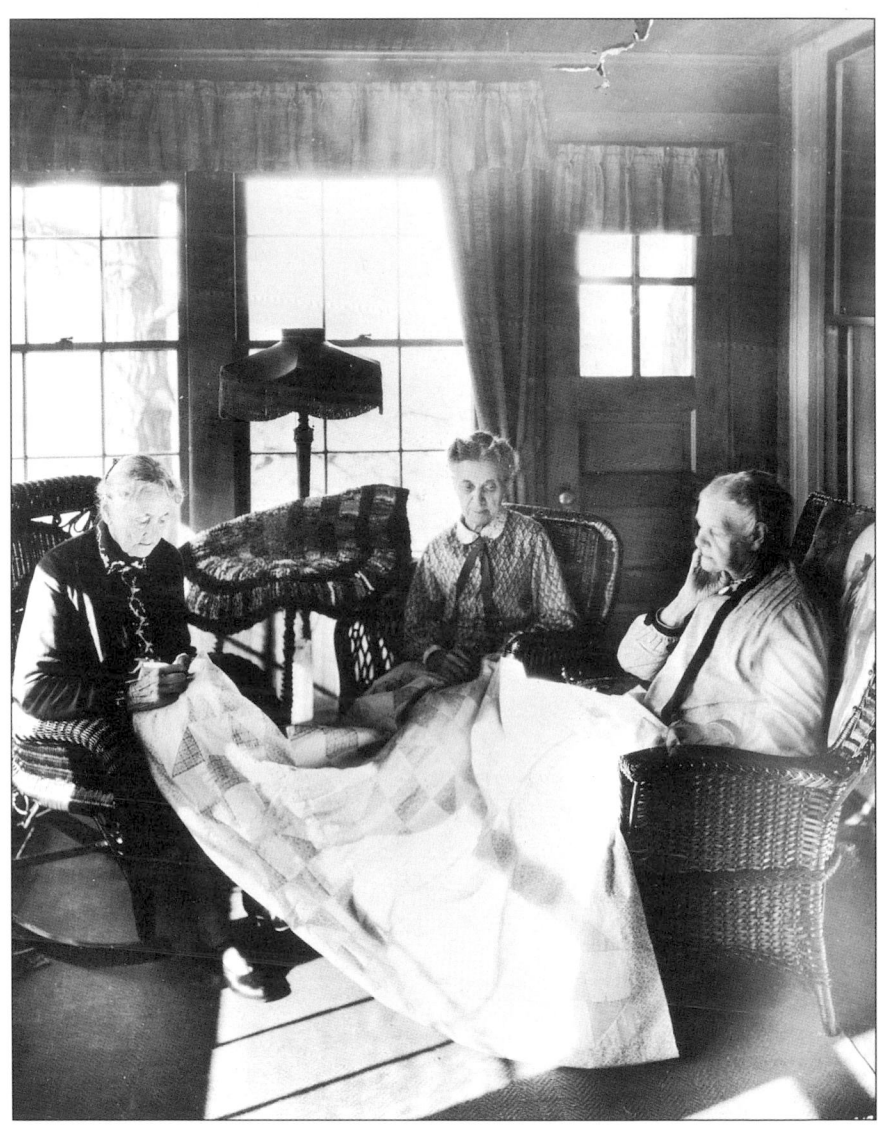

VOICES FROM THE QUILT
The three women in this photograph from 1925 seem to be listening for the story behind the quilt they hold as they complete its final stitches. (Minnesota Historical Society)

A QUILT'S WELCOME
A home appears more inviting when there is a quilt or two to greet you. These quilts, hung on the front porch of an Amish home in Intercourse, Pennsylvania, welcome neighbors and prospective quilt buyers with colors that rival a well-kept flower garden. (Photograph © Keith Baum/BaumsAway!)

democratic dream? What does it say about us? Did we inherit the dream or the illicit, unsettling racial relationship?

This sort of thing is not considered scholarly or academic or of consequence, these small footnotes. And perhaps rightly so. Of course, I loved the important, rigorous historical inquiry as well. What I think I wanted was both things, the silly and the sublime; which adds up to a whole picture, a grudgingly true past. And out of that past truth a present reality.

You could say I was having trouble linking the two.

I wished for history to be vital, alive with the occasional quirk of human nature (a little "seriojovial"); I imagined someone saying to me, *Finn, what ever gave you the idea that history was any sort of living thing? Really. Isn't that expectation just the least bit contradictory?*

Then Sam asked me to marry him.

It seemed to me a good idea.

Yet it somehow led me back to my educational concern, which was how to mesh halves into a whole, only in this case it was how to make a successful link of unmarried to married, man to woman, the merging of the roads before us. When Heathcliff ran away from Wuthering Heights, he left Cathy wild and sad, howl-

ing on the moors, *I am Heathcliff*, as if their love were so powerful, their souls so seamlessly mated, that no division existed for them, save the corporeal (though I tend to believe they got "together" at least once), which is of little consequence in the presence of the spirit.

All of which leaves me wondering, astonished, and a little put off. How does one accomplish such a fusion of selves? And, if the affection is that strong, how does one *avoid* it, leaving a little room for the person you once were? The balance of marriage, the delicate, gentle shifting of the polished scales.

Let me say that I like Sam tremendously. I love him truly.

The other good idea was spending the summer with my grandmother Hy Dodd and her sister Glady Joe Cleary. Their relationship with me is different from that with the other grandchildren; we share secrets. And I probably talk to them a little more than my cousins or their own children do. I think they have a lot to say and I am more than willing to hear it. All of it. Whatever strikes them as important.

To me, they are important.

So my days are now spent watching the quilters come and go, lazily eavesdropping on the hum of their conversation and drifting off into dreams on my great-aunt's generous porch; thinking about my Sam, my sweetheart. Or lying on my back, in the shade, in Aunt Glady's extravagant garden, removing the ice cubes from my tea, running them across my face, neck, and chest in an effort to cool down from the heat.

I could wander over to the Grasse swimming pool, but it is always so crowded. Sophia Richards says you never know who you'll meet there—as if I want to meet anyone. As if I am not already staying in a house that has quite a bit of "foot traffic."

The quilters have offered to make a bridal quilt in honor of my marriage, but I tell them to *Please continue with what you are doing as if I never arrived to stay for the summer.* Sometimes I say, *I can't think about that*

Perennial Favorites

DUTCH ROSE, DESIGN No. 307 — 15" Block. Brought to this country by early Dutch settlers, this pattern will delight the most discriminating quiltmaker. To cut pieces for one block, use Diagram No. 307A on page 6 for 8 pieces; 307B on page 10 for 16 pieces; 307C on page 10 for 4 pieces; and 307D on page 14 for 32 pieces. Multiply by number of blocks desired for additional pieces necessary to complete quilt.

ROCKINGHAM BEAUTY, DESIGN No. 404—15" Block. An old and very good pattern. Splendid when done in striking color combinations. To make one block, cut 16 pieces of Diagram No. 404A on page 6; 4 pieces of No. 404B on page 7; 1 piece of 404C on page 10; and 24 pieces of Diagram No. 404D on page 14. Multiply by number of blocks desired to obtain correct number of pieces for complete quilt.

FIVE POINTED STAR, DESIGN No. 204—9" Block. Done on a white background in solid colors this design is simplicity itself. Neat and colorful, goes well in any room. To make one block, cut 1 piece of Diagram No. 204A found on page 7; 2 pieces of 204B, 2 pieces of 204C, and 5 pieces of 204D found on page 14. Multiply by number of blocks desired to find number of pieces needed for complete quilt.

GRANDMA'S FLOWER GARDEN, DESIGN No. 304 —12" Block. A favorite of the '90's! Thousands of Americans grew up in homes where quilts of this design were used. Bright and cheerful when made from gayly colored prints. To make one block, cut 19 pieces of Diagram No. 304A found on page 10. For pieces for entire quilt, multiply by number of blocks needed.

STAR BOUQUET, DESIGN No. 202—18" Block. Very pretty indeed when made up in rainbow colors. Makes a good showing and is an ideal pattern for beginners. Permits thrifty use of small pieces of material. To make one block, cut 72 pieces of Diagram No. 202A found on page 6. To obtain required number of pieces for complete quilt, multiply by number of blocks needed.

CARE OF THE FINISHED QUILT

As soon as your new quilt is finished, air it well. Hang it by the top and bottom on a line or between 2 lines so that air can flow freely through it. This method keeps quilt "all square" to the world. Similar occasional airings are desirable throughout the life of your quilt. Contrary to the belief of some quilt-makers, it is not only permissible but advisable to launder or clean quilts occasionally. To launder, allow quilt to soak in lukewarm suds. Work up and down in water gently but do not rub or scrub. Rinse in lukewarm water, handling as before. Do not wring out water—simply squeeze quilt gently and hang dripping on line.

"Perennial Favorites"
This page from a vintage quilt pattern catalog illustrates the philosophy that time-honored quilt patterns never go out of style. The Grandma's Flower garden design it lists as "A favorite of the '90s!"—the 1890s, that is—is still being made by quilters young and old today.

now (as if anyone can think clearly in this peppery heat). I can see this puzzles them, makes them wonder what sort of girl it is who "cannot think about" her own wedding.

This amuses me as well, since, at age twenty-six, I have lost track of the sort of girl that I am. I used to be a young scholar; I am now an engaged woman. Not that you cannot be both—even I understand that— yet I cannot fathom who I think I am *at this time.* My aunt Glady told me recently that this strikes her as "healthy and sensible"—to take a minute or so for yourself, to take a little time to think.

The true source of my interest during this visit, this impasse in my own life, is Anna Neale, another one of the quilters and my aunt's oldest friend. Anna has promised me a long talk one day, she says, when

she is not so busy, when there is nothing else to do. But her time always seems occupied. She's remarkably beautiful, Anna Neale is. Even at seventy-three. She can turn heads.

We are all drawn to beauty. I think it is a beacon for us; makes us want to listen.

Well, I am ready to listen.

Instructions No. 1

What you need:

You need a large wooden frame and enough space to accommodate it. Put comfortable chairs around it, allowing for eight women of varying ages, weight, coloring, and cultural orientation. It is preferable that this large wood frame be located in a room in a house

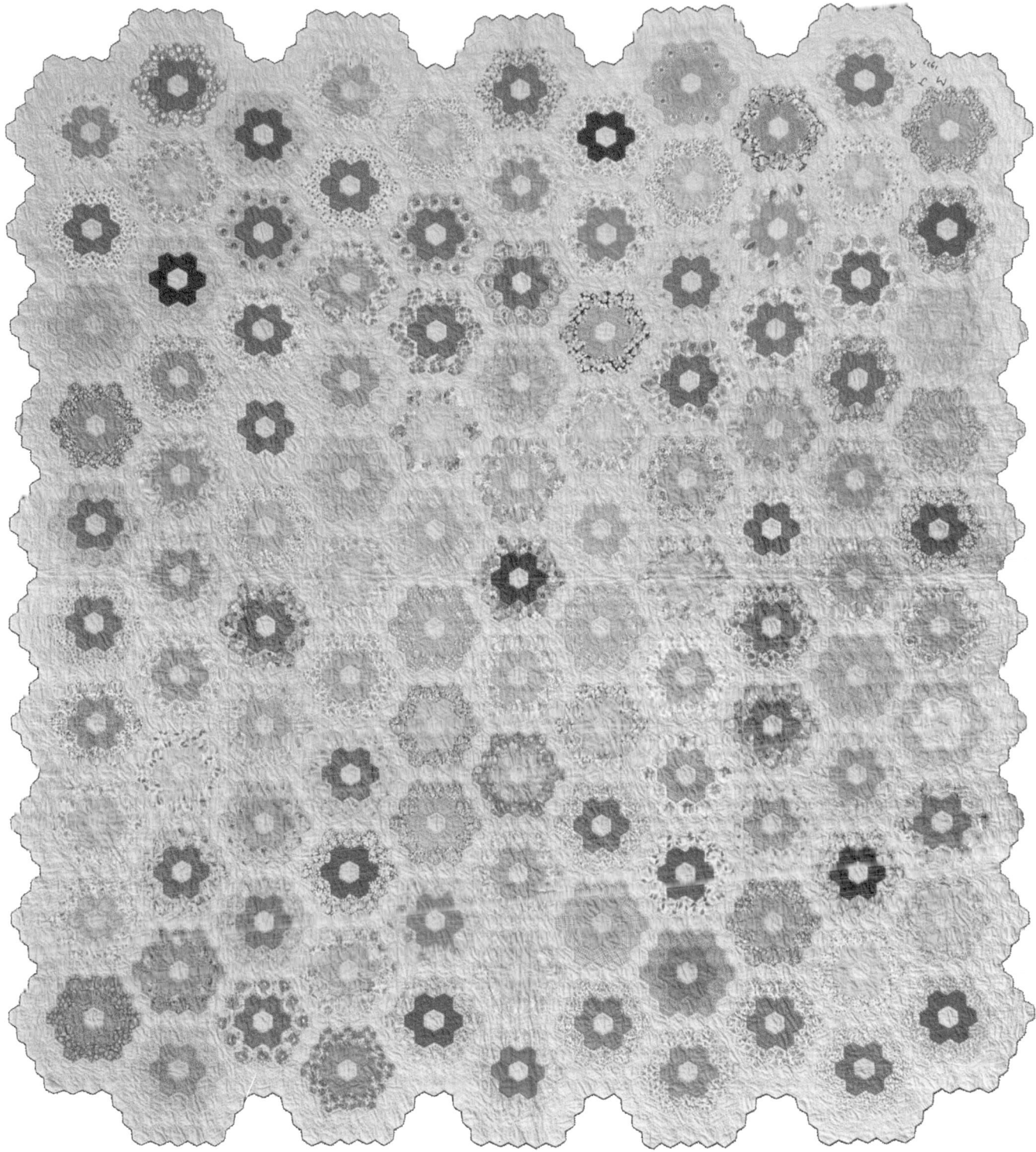

GRANDMOTHER'S FLOWER GARDEN
This popular pattern is made of small hexagons that are pieced together without an outside border, leaving an attractive scalloped edge. The Grandmother's Flower Garden design is thought to have originated shortly after World War I and soon became a staple of many quilters' repertoires; the example pictured here was made in 1937. (Minnesota Historical Society)

in Atwater or Los Banos or a small town outside Bakersfield called Grasse. It should be a place that gets a thick, moist blanket of tule fog in the winter and be hot as blazes in the summer. Fix plenty of lemonade. Cookies are a nice complement.

When you choose your colors, make them sympathetic to one another. Consider the color wheel of grammar school—primary colors, phenomena of light and dark; avoid antagonism of hues—it detracts from the pleasure of the work. Think of music as you orchestrate the shades and patterns; pretend that you are a conductor in a lush symphony hall, imagine the audience saying *Ooh* and *Ahh* as they applaud your work.

Patterns with tiny, precise designs always denote twentieth-century taste.

Your needles must be finely honed so you do not break the weave of your fabric. The ones from England are preferable. And plenty of good-quality thread, both to bind the pieces and adorn the quilt. Embroidery thread is required for the latter. You will need this to hold the work together for future generations. Unless you are interested in selling your quilt at an art fair or gallery, in which case the quilt will still need to be held together for generations of people you will never meet.

The women who circle the frame should be compatible. Their names are: Sophia, Glady Joe, Hy, Constance, Em, Corrina, Anna, and Marianna. Hyacinth and Gladiola Josephine are sisters, two years apart, and always called Hy and Glady Joe. Anna and Marianna are mother and daughter, seventeen years apart. Em, Sophia, and Corrina are all natives to Grasse, while Constance is a relative newcomer. When you have assembled the group, once a week for better than thirty-five years, give or take some latecomers, you will be ready to begin the traditional, free-form *Crazy Quilt*.

The *Crazy Quilt* was a fad of the nineteenth century and as such is not truly considered Art, yet still it has its devotees. It is comprised of remnants of material in numerous textures, colors; actually, you could not call the squares of a *Crazy Quilt* squares, since the stitched-together pieces are of all sizes and shapes. This is the pattern with the least amount of discipline and the greatest measure of emotion. Considering the eight quilters surrounding the frame in the room of the house in the small town outside Bakersfield called Grasse,

considering the more than thirty-five years it will reveal, perhaps some emerging images will be lambs or yellow roses or mermaids, entwined wedding rings or hearts in states of disrepair. You will find this work to be most revealing, not only in the material contributions to the quilt, but in who enjoys sewing them and who does not. This random piecing together.

More Instructions

What you should understand when undertaking the construction of a quilt is that it is comprised of spare time as well as excess material. Something left over from a homemade dress or a man's shirt or curtains for the kitchen window. It utilizes that which would normally be thrown out, "waste," and eliminates the extra, the scraps. And out of that which is left comes a new, useful object.

Take material from clothing that belongs to some family member or friend or lover (if you find yourself to be that sort of a girl). Bind them together carefully. Wonder at the disparity of your life. Finger the patches representing "lover" and meditate on the meaning of illicit love in early American society. Failing that, consider the meaning of the affair in today's time frame.

The Roanoke Island Company, founded by Sir Walter Raleigh in 1585, completely disappeared—all 117 men, women, and children—by 1590 with no one knowing exactly what took place during that five-year period, and a single word carved into a tree the only viable clue: CROATOAN. No historian has figured out what that means. This you will find as the genesis and recurring theme in America as founded by the English: that we are a people fraught with mysteries and clues; there are things that cannot be fathomed.

Do not forget that the Norse, Spanish, French, Italians, and god knows who else arrived before the English, relative latecomers to this place, and that the Indians stood on the shores, awaiting them all. These same Indians were exploited by the English, who were lazy and preferred to spend their time smoking tobacco on the banks of the James River rather than till the soil, expecting "someone else" to do it for them. Killing themselves by the end of the first winter because, as they emphatically told the Indians, *We are not farmers. We are explorers*, then demanded their provisions. Some say this is where the seeds of slavery were sown. An institution the English were not devious enough

MIXED BAG

The Crazy quilt was typically made from the most luxurious pieces of fabric in the quilter's scrap bag, featured extensive embroidery, and was finished with elaborate stitchery. This Crazy quilt, circa 1890, is made up of forty-nine blocks that feature an embroidered anchor, a spider in a web, flowers, and cherries. (Courtesy of Washington County MN Historical Society, photograph by Tomy O'Brien)

to come up with on their own, instead adopting it from the Spanish, who had been dealing in African flesh for a number of years. But that is another story.

Consider that women came across the Atlantic from the beginning and were not allowed to vote until 1920. A quick calculation leaves you wondering about those hundreds of years in between. You are curious about their power, their spheres of influence. Most historians agree that the first president voted in by the women was a washout, a different sort of man than Washington, Lincoln, Jefferson, and so on. Men can take credit for those presidents.

Recall that women who came to newly colonized America often outlived their husbands and that it was not uncommon, in those early Virginia days, for them to be widowed and inherit, remarry, be widowed and inherit, remarry, and so on. This, you would think, may have been a frightening cycle to a number of men in the area, never knowing when their number was up, so to speak. But with so few careers open to women at the time, they simply made the best with what they had to work with. Not unlike fashioning a quilt from scraps, if you think about it. And there weren't that many of them, proportionally speaking. With that sort of social arrangement, you find yourself wondering if all these husband deaths were strictly due to natural causes; but to conjecture such a thought, without historical verification, would be to assume the worst about the early settlers. No reputable historian would suggest such a thing: duplicitous, untrustworthy, murderous women. Not just any women, but *wives*.

She used whatever material she had at hand and if she was too overburdened with work she could ask her husband, sweetly, with sugar in her voice, to please, please look into acquiring an indentured servant. England, experiencing a bit of an economic crisis, had a surplus of unemployed citizens it was not much interested in caring for, and Virginia, Tidewater, and Maryland took on the look of an acceptable repository. Ah, but that is to confuse convicts with indentures and, really, they are not the same. An indentured servant is more like a slave, whereas a convict is more like a caged man. Different. You see.

Later, a turn in England's financial fortunes led to a drop-off of people interested in coming to America as servants, what with renewed opportunity at home (and that unholy Atlantic crossing), and an attempt to fill the resulting American employment gap paved the way for African-American slavery. But that is another story.

The nineteenth century brought an explosion of ideas to the concept of the quilt, of a woman's political voice. Not to mention the domestic conflicts of the Revolutionary War, followed by the Civil War (with one or two small—by comparison—skirmishes in between). Ignore the fact that the Revolution still left some unequal and the Civil War had a rather specific definition of brother against brother, neglecting to include color or gender. That, too, is another story.

Your concern might be trying to reduce your chosen quilt topic to more manageable dimensions. For example, the Revolutionary War could be defined as a bloody betrayal. One can almost hear the voice of Mother England crying, "But you are mine. An extension of me. You promised to be faithful, to send back your riches and keep me in a style to which I have become accustomed." America's answer something like: I need my space. It isn't that I am not fond of you. We can still maintain a friendly trading relationship."

There is the Civil War, which is a conflict of the blood tie. No one fights dirtier or more brutally than blood; only family knows its own weakness, the exact placement of the heart. The tragedy is that one can still love with the force of hatred. Feel infuriated that once you are born to another, that kinship lasts through life and death, immutable, unchanging, no matter how great the misdeed or betrayal. Blood cannot be denied, and perhaps that is why we fight tooth and claw, because we cannot, being only human, put asunder what God has joined together.

Women were witness to Abraham Lincoln's assassination. Find some quality silk and cotton in red, white, and blue. Cut white stars in the evening as you sit on your summer porch. Appliqué the letters that spell out your name, your country, your grief. Stitch across the quilt a flag held in the beak of a dove. Ponder the fact that you could not vote for the man but will defy any male citizen who will not allow you your measure of sorrow at the president's sudden death. Say something in cloth about the Union lasting, preserved. Listen to the men expound their personal satisfaction in glory of the vote. Listen to them express surprise that you, too, would like to vote and be heard. They might say, *This is not your concern*, and conclude that perhaps you are too idle at home and should consider having another child.

SECRETS SHARED

A quilting bee is the perfect opportunity to swap quilting patterns and fabric scraps. Any interesting gossip, however, must wait until all of the husbands have left the room. This photograph from 1925 features eight industrious quilters and one stubborn husband. (Photograph by the Minneapolis Star-Journal, Minnesota Historical Society)

Save your opinions for your quilt. Put your heart and voice into it. Cast your ballot; express your feelings regarding industrialization, emancipation, women's suffrage, your love of family.

Send away for silk ribbon printed with black-lined photolithographs. Try your hand at doing these ink drawings yourself. Experiment with the colors newly available from nineteenth-century factories: peacock blue, scarlet, jade green, eggplant, and amber. Save a scrap of velvet. For texture.

As the nineteenth century draws to a close, be sure to express your gratitude for the "improvements" in your life; you can drive your own buggy, attend college, or work in a textile factory in Lowell, Massachusetts. And do not forget the popular magazines like *Peterson's* or *Godey's Lady's Book*, which encourage the

decorative quilt over the story quilt (the quilt with a voice), as it can safely be displayed outside the bedroom without offense. Place it in the parlor. Simply to work a pattern and color with no ulterior thought is the mark of a woman of leisure and reflects well on her husband.

You want to keep these things in mind: history and family. How they are often inseparable. In the twentieth century you may feel that all those things that went before have little to do with you, that you are made immune to the past by the present day: All those dead people and conflicts and ideas—why, they are only stories we tell one another. History and politics and conflict and rebellion and family and betrayal.

Think about it.

31 Quilt Designs

by TAYLOR·MADE
with
COMPLETE CUTTING CHARTS
AND EASY TO FOLLOW DIRECTIONS
FOR
MAKING LUXURIOUS, LONG-WEARING
QUILTS and COMFORTS

How <u>Not</u> to Make a
Prize-Winning Quilt

By Ami Simms

AMI SIMMS WAS bitten by the quilting bug in 1975 when she went to visit an Old Order Amish community in northern Indiana as part of her undergraduate research. A group of Amish women had invited her to join them around their quilting frame, and Simms has been a quilter ever since—even though, her Amish friend Ida told her later, all of Ami's stitches at that first quilting were taken out as soon as she had gone.

Simms, a resident of Flint, Michigan, is now an accomplished quilter with almost one hundred finished quilts under her belt. She is also the author of several quilting books including *How to Improve Your Quilting Stitch* and *Every Trick in the Book* and is the founder of The Worst Quilt in the World Contest.

This excerpt from *How Not to Make a Prize Winning Quilt* demonstrates why the seam-ripper is often a beginning quilter's best friend. But the joy of quilting does not need to be hampered by a few uneven stitches. As Simms writes, "The ultimate measure of your quiltmaking success is not what anyone else thinks of your quilt, but rather what *you* think of it." Beauty is truly in the eye of the beholder.

■ ■ ■

My first quilt show was a real eye-opener. I'd made a handful of quilts but I guess I was no expert. Watching the ladies handling the quilts with white gloves, I thought they all had some kind of communicable skin disease. My friend and I had made the pilgrimage to Ft. Wayne, Indiana, for the 11th Annual National Quilting Association Show. I had taught her everything I knew about quilting the week before, and we decided to go and hobnob with the other quilters.

The instant we walked into the show I knew we were out of their league. In fact, I was sure we weren't even playing the same game. We loved every quilt we saw and couldn't for the life of us figure out why they all weren't wearing ribbons.

After about an hour we risked catching whatever the poor women in the white gloves were afflicted with and asked one to explain how the quilts had been judged. She shared some of the finer points of quilt judging, of which we were totally ignorant. She explained that stitches should be small and even, seams flat, corners square, and bindings fully stuffed. She continued with admonitions against loose stitches, crooked quilting, inconsistent grainline, and non-matching thread. Then she started in on

STATE FAIR PRIZEWINNER
This vintage quilt design booklet, which comes with full-size cutting charts, promises that if you follow the patterns inside carefully, you, too, can win a coveted blue ribbon.

"DAY OF THE QUILT SHOW"
A quilt show can be an inspiring yet overwhelming place for fledgling quilters. While they may leave the exhibition with a head full of ideas for future projects, they may also leave confused as to why all the beautiful quilts they saw weren't wearing blue ribbons. This award-worthy painting by artist Sandi Wickersham of Purcellville, Virginia, portrays the excitement of a local quilt show. (Artwork © Sandi Wickersham)

points that don't meet, seams that are pressed to the "light" instead of to the "dark," sloppy miters, and wobbly borders.

If you've ever seen the plastic doggies that sit on the back window ledges of cars and bob their heads up and down as they go down the road, then you'll know exactly what we looked like. The more she explained, the less we understood. Our eyes glazed over and we nodded our heads like plastic doggies. We thanked her and tried to extricate ourselves as she was getting into a long discourse on how it was preferable to have two evenly spaced seams on the back of a quilt instead of one ugly one running right down the middle. (Heaven forbid!) We agreed enthusiastically, smiled, and waved good-bye.

Thankfully, we made it behind the first full-size quilt out of earshot before doubling over with laughter. Maybe the gloves indicated some mental condition: Chronic Picky-itis.

We continued with the rest of the show, admiring the quilts and wondering how the poor souls who entered them would react to learning that the judges were delusional. I figured those gals in the white gloves were also a few inches short of a yard! It was either that, or I was an expert in how <u>not</u> to make a prize-winning quilt. Ah-ha. . . .

Lesson One:

If Nothing Falls Off You're Doing OK

My first quilt came off the cover of a craft magazine. I should have left it there. Instead of templates, piecing diagrams, and pages of instructions, this magazine had little patches drawn on miniature graph paper next to 12 words of "how-to." It was all the way in the back of the magazine sandwiched between ads for hearing aids and support hose.

The reader was supposed to enlarge it. Now there's a concept. You make a bunch of big squares that look like their little squares and re-draw their lines on your paper. Not very accurate. I once made a pair of pants using one of these enlarge-it-yourself patterns and by the time I was finished it had three legs and a lapel!

My quilt pattern was called Converging Blocks and it looked a little like bargello, if you squinted your eyes and stepped way back. Like Montana. The magazine featured it in shades of brown. I went way out on the creativity limb and made mine in blues.

I had a surprisingly easy time of it. The pieces went together perfectly. Remember, I had only really seen three real quilts in my life: two made out of recycled pajamas and boxer shorts, and the trampoline the Amish women were sewing on. I wasn't that concerned with corners meeting and seams lying flat. When I came to the end of a row I just whacked off whatever hung off or took a pleat. I figured if I shook the top and nothing fell off I was doing pretty good!

Lesson Two:

Make Bigger Stitches; It Takes Less Time

My Amish friend, Ida, ever the patient teacher, encouraged me. She looked at my efforts, crossed her fingers behind her back, and told me I was doing just fine. When my quilt top was ready to quilt she was there with a handful of her friends and relatives to help.

We put the quilt in frame and quilted as far as we could reach all the way around the outside before the day was over. Those Amish ladies were good, but I was much faster. You can be faster when your stitches are an inch and a half longer than anyone else's.

We rolled the quilt up on the long stretcher bars of the frame, wrapped newspaper around it, tied a red flag to the end, and jammed it in my Chevette for the drive home. Back at school I set up a makeshift quilting frame and injured my fingers in between a full class load, a part-time job, and pestering the poor guy I would eventually marry who lived halfway across the state. . . .

A short time before the quilt was actually finished I gave it to my parents for their 30th wedding anniversary, starting the beloved and practical tradition of giving quilts not entirely finished. It's much less stressful. I figured Mom could sew on the binding herself.

My parents loved the quilt, but then again I'm an only child. They really were so proud of me. And rightly so. I had just about finished a full-size and nearly rectangular quilt in a scant six months. It pays to make big stitches. It goes so much faster.

Lesson Three:

Bite Off More Than You Can Chew

By the time I began my student teaching some four months later I was ready for another quilt. I had heard

Star quilt
Beginning quilters be warned: Any seasoned quiltmaker will tell you that it can be quite challenging to perfectly stitch together the myriad diamond-shaped pieces that make up the Star quilt. (Photograph © Jerry Irwin)

somewhere that a young woman about to be married should have a dozen quilts. Finished ones. I have no idea who made this up, but the wedding was less than a year away and I was 12 quilts behind. Time to get cracking!

Besides, I thought if I invested the time and energy to make a quilt, I'd be more inclined to make the bed, and my true nature would be hidden from my husband forever. This actually did work—for about two weeks.

Like most beginning quilters I picked something small and simple: a Lone Star. That's 968 diamonds for those of you who are counting, cut and stitched with precision by a rank beginner. And without pins. It measured 96" x 118" when it was finally finished— at least on two sides. And, no, I didn't trim off any of the points after I joined the diamonds. Seeing as I didn't press the seams I had no idea they were even there!

Lesson Four:

If Something Goes Wrong It Must Be The Pattern

I student-taught in a small town in southwestern Michigan that was linked to the rest of the world (Kalamazoo) by a highway prone to collecting snow drifts. When it snowed and the wind blew, nobody moved. That winter we had 12 snow days in a row— the worst winter in 20 years. By the time we got back to school we had to wear name tags.

I spent my snow days purposefully piecing my Lone Star. My student model Singer, a reject from some home-ec class, wheezed and burped on the kitchen table as I stitched. All day long. I fed hundreds of diamonds between the presser foot and the feed dogs, and when I was all done I had this little, itty, bitty, very lonely star that barely touched the edges of the bed. I was shocked.

All that work and it didn't look a thing like the grown-up star in the book. And then I realized that the pattern was wrong. The author of the book was a vicious woman who was deliberately out to confuse me and ruin my quilt. Her diamonds were drawn with

double lines and I picked the wrong line! Cutting on the sewing line wasn't bad enough, didn't she know I had a fat presser foot and my quarter-inch was closer to a third?!

Lesson Five:

If It Doesn't Fit, Pull On It Or Cut It Off

As soon as the snow melted I drove down to Indiana to show Ida. She was going to help me "set in" the background and she'd tell me if my star was worth saving. She said we could save it with a little extra fabric. Luckily, the sheet I had bought to "set in" was a full. No skimping here.

I watched my friend stitch and pivot my little star's first point. I was in the presence of greatness. She didn't catch her finger once, and she was using a treadle. I went home to attack the other seven points.

Though lacking expertise, I was brimming with determination. I stretched and flattened the other points into submission. If something didn't quite fit, I just yanked it into place or cut it off.

Lesson Six:

Don't Worry, It'll Quilt Out

My top was perfect. It covered an entire bed and then some. I had even gotten used to the puny size of the star. I drove back to Indiana to show Ida, nearly bursting with self-congratulation.

Somehow during the ride down, my magnificent Lone Star became deformed. I don't know if the radio was too loud or there wasn't enough air in the bag, but when we flapped it out on the bed it had a belly big enough to hide a cat The rest of the quilt wasn't sitting too flat either

There was way too much quilt around the outside edge and there seemed to be large pockets of air trapped underneath. No sooner did we burp one side than the air pockets redistributed to another! I was devastated.

Then I heard those immortal words: "Don't worry, it'll quilt out."

QUILTING IN COMFORT
A quilting hoop allows this woman easy and accurate stitches as she works on her Grandmother's Flower Garden quilt. It also serves as a table for a pair of scissors and extra thread. (Photograph © J. C. Allen & Son)

The Quilter's Apprentice

By Jennifer Chiaverini

JENNIFER CHIAVERINI'S FIRST quilt was a nine-block sampler that she duplicated from the pages of a booklet entitled "Teach Yourself to Quilt." She has since developed her quilting skills with the help of countless instruction books and magazines and the support of her many on-line quilting friends.

Her career as an author has developed as well: *The Quilter's Apprentice* is the first of three novels in the Elm Creek Quilts series, which traces the lives of a close-knit group of quilters. It is followed by Chiaverini's other books *Round Robin* and *The Cross Country Quilters*. Currently making a home with her husband and son in Madison, Wisconsin, Chiaverini says that she wrote *The Quilter's Apprentice* as a gift for all the quilters she has known through the years.

This excerpt from the book introduces us to Sarah McClure and her soon-to-be quilt teacher, Sylvia Compson. Sarah and her husband, Matt, are new to Waterford, Pennsylvania, and she is in search of a job. When Matt's landscaping business takes the two of them to visit Elm Creek Manor, Sarah cannot resist poking around the impressive mansion and discovers a beautiful quilt in the sitting room—she also discovers the cantankerous personality of gifted quiltmaker and honored member of the American Quilters' Society, Mrs. Sylvia Compson.

■ ■ ■

Sarah's heart leaped when she returned home to find the answering machine's light blinking. A message. Maybe Waterford College had called about that admissions counselor job. She let her packages fall to the floor and scrambled for the button. Or maybe it was from PennCellular Corporation. That would be even better.

"Hi, Sarah. It's me."

Matt.

"I'm calling from the office, but I was up at Elm Creek Manor this morning, and—well, I guess it can wait until I get home. Hope you don't have any plans for tomorrow. See you tonight. Love you."

As the tape rewound, Sarah left her backpack on the hallway floor and brought the groceries into the kitchen. What was it that could wait until he got home? She considered phoning Matt to see what was going on, but decided not to interrupt his work. Instead she put away the groceries and went into the living room. She opened the sliding door just enough to allow a breeze to circulate through the duplex, then stretched out on the sofa and listened to the rain.

What should she do now? She'd done the laundry the day before and wouldn't have to start dinner for a while. Maybe she could call one of her friends from school. No, at this time of day they would all be working or busy with their graduate school classes and research.

Funny how things had turned out. In college she had been the one with clear goals and direction, taking all the right classes and participating in all the right extracurricular activities and summer internships. Her friends had often remarked that their own career plans seemed vague or nonexistent in comparison. And now they were going places while she sat around the house with nothing to do.

She rolled over on her side and stared at the blank television screen. Nothing would be on now—nothing good, anyway. She almost wished she had some homework to do. If only she had picked a different major—marketing, or management, maybe. Something in the sciences would have been even better. But in high school Sarah's guidance counselor had told her that there would always be jobs for accountants, and she had taken those words to heart. She had been the only freshman in her dorm who knew from the first day of classes what major she was going to declare at the end of the year. It had seemed so self-indulgent to ask herself if she enjoyed accounting, if she thought she would find it a fulfilling career. If only she had listened to her heart instead of her guidance counselor. Ultimately, though, she knew she had no one but herself to blame now that she had no marketable job skills beyond bean counting.

Suddenly exasperated with herself, she shoved the whining voices from her mind. True, she didn't have a job, but she didn't have to mope and complain like the voice of doom. That was what her mother would do. What Sarah needed was something to keep herself occupied until a job came along. Moving into the duplex had kept her too busy to worry for a couple of weeks; maybe she could join a book club or take a course up at Waterford College.

Then her thoughts returned to the quilt she had seen in the shop window earlier that day. She jumped up from the sofa and retrieved her backpack from the hallway. The quilt shop's class schedule was still there, a bit damp from her rainy walk home from the bus stop. Sarah unfolded it and smoothed out the creases, studying the course names, dates, times, and prices.

Her heart sank. The costs seemed reasonable, but even reasonable expenses were too much when she hadn't seen a paycheck in more than two months. Like so many other things, quilting lessons would have to wait until the McClures were a dual-income family. But the more Sarah thought about it, the more she liked the idea. A quilt class would give her a chance to meet people, and a handmade quilt might make the duplex seem more like a home. She would talk to Matt about it. Maybe they could come up with the money somehow.

She decided to bring it up over supper that evening. "Matt," she began. "There's something I've been thinking about all day."

Matt took a second helping of corn and grinned. "You mean my phone message? I'm surprised you didn't ask about it sooner. Usually you hate it when I keep you in suspense."

Sarah paused. She had forgotten all about it. "That's right. You said you had to talk to me about something."

"First, though, do you have any plans for tomorrow?"

Something in his tone made her wary. "Why?"

"Yes or no?"

"I'm afraid to answer until I know why you're asking."

"Sheesh. So suspicious." But he put down his fork and hesitated a moment. "I spent the day up at Elm Creek Manor inspecting the trees. Not a trace of Dutch elm disease anywhere. I don't know how they managed it."

"I hope you didn't get caught in the rain."

"Actually, as soon as the thunder started, Mrs. Compson made me come inside. She even fixed me lunch."

"You're kidding. She didn't make you cook it yourself?"

"No." He chuckled. "She's a pretty good cook, too. While I was eating, we kind of got to talking. She wants you to come see her tomorrow."

"What? What for? Why would she want to see me?"

"She didn't say exactly. She said she wanted to tell you in person."

"I'm not going. Tell her I can't come. Tell her I'm busy."

Matt's face assumed the expression it always did

QUILTS MAKE A HOUSE A HOME
Colorful quilts can brighten any home, whether they cover a bed, hang on a wall, or are thrown over the back of a chair. This House quilt was created by Mary Lou Fischer of Fulton, New York. (Photograph © Dianne Dietrich Leis)

AGE BEFORE BEAUTY

In most cases, a quilter must put in years of practice before she can produce a masterpiece of method and beauty. When she has perfected the art of the craft, she is ready to pass on her expertise to the next generation of quiltmakers. (Photograph © J. C. Allen & Son)

when he knew he was about to get in trouble. "I can't. I already told her you'd come in with me tomorrow morning."

"Why'd you do that? Call her and tell her—tell her something. Say I have a dentist appointment."

"I can't. She doesn't have a phone, remember?"

"Matt—"

"Think of it this way. It's a lot cooler out there than in town, right? You could get out of this heat for a while."

"I'd rather stay home and turn on the air-conditioning."

"Oh, come on, honey, what would it hurt?" He put on his most effective beseeching expression. "She's an important client. Please?"

Sarah frowned at him, exasperated.

"Please?"

She rolled her eyes. "Oh, all right. Just, please, next time, ask me before you commit me to something."

"Okay. Promise."

Sarah shook her head and sighed. She knew better.

The next morning was sunny and clear, not nearly as humid as it had been before yesterday's rainstorm. "Why would she want to see me?" Sarah asked again as Matt drove them to Mrs. Compson's home.

"For the fourth time, Sarah, I don't know. You'll find out when get there."

"She's probably going to demand an apology for

snooping around her house." Sarah tried to remember the exchange in the sewing room. She'd apologized when Mrs. Compson caught her, hadn't she? "I don't think I actually said I was sorry. I think I was too surprised. She probably dragged me out here to give me a lecture on manners."

Her stomach twisted into a nervous knot that tightened as the truck pulled into the gravel driveway behind the manor.

"You could apologize before she asks you to," Matt said as he parked the truck. "Old people like apologies and polite stuff like that."

"Yeah. I hear they also love being referred to as 'old people,'" Sarah muttered. She climbed out of the truck and slammed the door. But maybe Matt had a point. She trailed behind him as he led the way to the back door.

Mrs. Compson opened it on the first knock. "So, you're here. Both of you. Well, come on in." She left the door open and they followed her into the foyer.

"Mrs. Compson," Matt called after her as she walked ahead of them down a wide, dimly lit hallway. "I was planning to work in the orchard today. Is there anything else you'd like me to do first?"

She stopped and turned around. "No, the orchard is fine. Sarah may remain here with me." Matt and Sarah exchanged a puzzled glance. "Oh, don't worry. I won't work her too hard this morning. She'll see you at lunchtime."

Matt turned to Sarah, uncertain. "Sound okay to you?"

Sarah shrugged and nodded. She'd assumed that Mrs. Compson would want her to come in, make her apology, and leave, but if the woman wanted to drag things out . . . Sarah steeled herself. Well, Mrs. Compson *was* an important client.

With one last, uncertain smile, Matt turned and left the way they came. Sarah watched him go, then faced the old woman squarely. "Mrs. Compson," she said firmly, trying to sound regretful but not nervous, "I wanted to apologize for going into your sitting room with my lemonade and touching your quilt without permission. I shouldn't have done it and I'm sorry."

Mrs. Compson gave her a bemused stare. "Apology accepted." She turned and motioned for Sarah to follow.

Confused, Sarah trailed behind her as they approached a T intersection and turned right into an adjoining hallway. Wasn't that enough of an apology for her? What else was Sarah supposed to say?

The hallway opened into a large foyer, and Sarah slowly took in a breath. Even with the floor-to-ceiling windows covered by heavy draperies, she could tell how splendid the entryway could be if it were properly cared for. The floor was made of black marble, and to Sarah's left were marble steps leading down to twelve-foot-tall heavy wooden double doors. Oil paintings and mirrors in intricately carved frames lined the walls. Across the room was a smaller set of double doors, and a third set was on the wall to their right. In the corner between them a wooden staircase began; the first five steps were semicircular and led to a wedge-shaped landing from which a staircase climbed to the second-story balcony encircling the room. Looking up, Sarah could see another staircase continuing in a similar fashion to the third floor, and an enormous crystal chandelier hanging from the frescoed ceiling far above.

Mrs. Compson crossed the floor, carefully descended the marble steps, and waving off Sarah's efforts to assist, slowly pushed open one of the heavy doors.

Sarah followed her outside and tried not to gawk like a tourist. They stood on a wide stone veranda that ran the entire length of the front of the mansion. White columns supported a roof far overhead. Two stone staircases began at the center of the veranda, gracefully arcing away from each other and forming a half circle as they descended to the ground. The driveway encircled a large sculpture of a rearing horse; a second look told Sarah that it was a fountain choked with leaves and rainwater. Only that and the road leading from the driveway interrupted the green lawn that flowed from the manor to the distant trees.

Mrs. Compson eyed Sarah as she took all this in. "Impressed? Hmph." She stepped inside and reappeared with a broom, which she handed to Sarah. "Of course you are. Everyone is, the first time they see the place. At least they used to be, when we used to have visitors, before the estate went to pieces."

Sarah stood there uncertainly, looking from the broom to Compson and back.

"At least you came dressed for work, not like last time." Mrs. Compson gestured, first waving her arm to the north end of the veranda and then to the south. "Take care of the whole thing, and do a thorough job.

Don't neglect the dead leaves in the corners. I'll be back later." She moved toward the open doorway.

"Wait," Sarah called after her. "I think there's been a mistake. I can't sweep your porch."

Mrs. Compson turned and frowned at her. "A girl your age doesn't know how to sweep?"

"It's not that. I know how to sweep, but I—"

"Afraid of a bit of hard work, are you?"

"No, it's just that I think there's been a misunderstanding. You seem to think I work for Matt's company, but I don't."

"Oh. So they fired you, did they?"

"Of course not. They didn't fire me. I've never worked for Matt's company.

"If that's so, why did you accompany him that first time?"

"It was on the way. He was driving me home from a job interview."

"Hmph. Very well, then. Sweep the veranda anyway. If you're looking for work, I'd say you've found some. Just be glad I didn't ask you to mow the lawn."

Sarah gaped at her. "You know, you're really something." She threw down the broom and thrust her fists onto her hips. "I tried to apologize, tried to be polite, but you're just the rudest, the—the—if you had asked nicely I might have swept your porch as a favor to you, and to Matt, but—"

Mrs. Compson was grinning at her.

"What's so funny? You think being rude is funny?"

The old woman shrugged, clearly amused, which only irritated Sarah more. "I was beginning to wonder if you had any backbone at all."

"Believe me, I do," Sarah said through clenched teeth. She spun around and stormed down the nearest staircase.

"Wait," Mrs. Compson called. "Sarah, please, just a moment."

Sarah thought of Matt's contract, sighed, and stopped on the bottom step. She turned around to find Mrs. Compson preparing to come down the stairs after her. Sarah then realized there was no handrail, and the stone wall was worn too smooth for a secure grip. Mrs. Compson stumbled, and instinctively Sarah put out her arms as if to steady her, though she was too far away to make any difference if Mrs. Compson fell.

"All right," Sarah said. "I'm not going anywhere. You don't have to chase me."

Mrs. Compson shook her head and came down the stairs anyway. "I really could use some more help around here," she said, breathing heavily from exertion. "I'll pay you, of course."

"I'm looking for a real job. I went to college. I have a degree."

"Of course you do. Of course you do. But you could work for me until you find a better job. I won't mind if you need to leave early sometimes for job interviews."

She paused for a reply, but Sarah just looked at her, stone-faced.

"I don't know anybody else, you see," Mrs. Compson continued, and to Sarah's astonishment, her voice faltered. "I'm planning to sell the estate, and I need someone to help me collect my late sister's personal belongings and take an inventory of the manor's contents for auction. There are so many rooms, and I can't even imagine what could be in the attic, and I have trouble with stairs."

"You're going to sell the estate?"

The old woman shook her head. "A home so big and empty would be a burden. I have a place of my own, in Sewickley." Her lips twisted until they resembled a wry smile, but it looked as if she were out of practice. "I know what you're thinking. 'Work for this crotchety old thing? Never in a million years.'"

Sarah tried to compose her features so that her expression wouldn't give anything else away.

"I know I can be difficult sometimes, but I can try to be—" Mrs. Compson pursed her lips and glanced away as if searching for the proper adjective. "More congenial. What would it take to persuade you?"

Sarah studied her, then shook her head. "I'll need some time to think about it."

"Very well. You may remain here or in the kitchen if you like, or feel free to explore the grounds. The orchards are to the west, beyond the barn, and the gardens—what remains of them—are to the north. When you've decided, you may join me in the west sitting room. I believe you already know where that is." With that, she turned and made her way up the stairs and into the manor.

Sarah shook her head in disbelief as she watched Mrs. Compson go. When she said she needed some time to think about the offer, she'd meant a few days, not a few minutes. Then again, she had already made up her mind. Wait until Matt heard about this. As soon as he stopped laughing Sarah would get him to take her home, and with any luck she'd never have to see that strange old woman again.

Her eyes scanned the front of the manor. Mrs. Compson was right; she was impressed with the place. Who wouldn't be? But she doubted she could tolerate an employer like Mrs. Compson in order to work there. She was impressed, not masochistic. She walked around the tree-lined north side of the building and the west wing. She walked briskly, but it still took her ten minutes to reach the barn and another five to reach the orchard, where she found Matt retrieving some tools from the back of the pickup.

"You aren't going to believe this," she greeted him. "Mrs. Compson needs someone to help her get the manor ready for sale and she wants to hire me."

But Matt didn't burst into laughter as she had expected. Instead he set down his tool kit and leaned against the tailgate. "That's great, honey. When do you start?"

For a moment Sarah was too surprised to do anything but blink at him. "When do I start?"

"You're going to help her, aren't you?"

"I wasn't planning to," she managed to say.

"Why not? Why wouldn't you want the job?"

"It should be obvious. She hasn't been exactly nice to me, as you very well know."

"Don't you feel sorry for her?"

"Of course I feel sorry for her, but that doesn't mean I want to spend every day working with her."

"That's got to be better than moping around the house all day, right?"

"Not necessarily. If I'm sweeping porches around here, I won't be sending out résumés and going on interviews."

"I'm sure you could work something out."

"Matt, you don't get it. I've invested years in my career. I think I'm a little overqualified for cleaning up a house."

"I thought the whole idea was to start fresh."

"There's starting fresh and then there's starting over at the very bottom. There are limits."

Matt shrugged. "I don't see any. Honest work is honest work."

Sarah stared at him, perplexed. He had always been

"Mother's Treasures"
The youngster pictured on this Victorian trading card along with all the quilting essentials looks ready and willing to pick up a needle and thread. Some quiltmakers say that you're never too young—or too old—to learn how to quilt as long as you have a good teacher.

the first to point out that her career was her business, but now here he was practically pressuring her into a job that didn't even require a high school diploma. "Matt, if I take this job, my mother will have a fit."

"Why does it matter what your mother thinks? Besides, she wouldn't care. If anything, she'd be glad you're helping out an old lady."

Sarah started to reply, then held back the words and shook her head. If he only knew. She could almost hear that familiar chorus of shrill "I told you so's" already. If she took this job, she'd prove that her mother had been right all along when she'd insisted that leaving State College for Matt's sake would send Sarah's career into an inevitable spiral of downward mobility.

Then suspicion crept into her thoughts. "Matt, what's going on?"

"Nothing's going on. What do you mean?"

"First you brought me out here after my interview. Then, without checking with me first, you promised her that I'd come see her. You didn't look at all surprised when I told you she offered me a job, and now you're pushing me to take it. You knew she was going to offer me this job, didn't you?"

"I didn't know for sure. I mean, she hinted, but she didn't come right out and say it." He looked at the ground. "I guess I like the idea better than you do."

Exasperated, Sarah struggled for something to say. "Why?"

"It would be nice if we worked at the same place. We'd get to see more of each other."

"That might be part of it, but what else?"

Matt sighed, took off his cap, and ran his fingers through his curly hair until it looked even more unruly than usual. "You're going to think I'm being silly."

Silly was more benign than the adjectives Sarah considered using. "Maybe, but tell me anyway."

"Okay, but don't laugh." He tried to smile, but his eyes were sad. "Mrs. Compson, well, she reminds me of my mom. Same mannerisms, same way of dressing; she even looks kind of the same. Except her age, of course. I mean, I know she's probably old enough to be our grandmother . . ."

"Oh, Matt."

"It's just that, well, my mom's probably out there all alone somewhere, and I'd like to think that if some young couple had a chance to look out for her they'd take it."

If your mother's out there alone, it's her own fault for running out on you and your dad, Sarah thought, pressing her lips together to hold back the automatic response. She went to him and hugged him tightly. How could Matt remember his mother's mannerisms? Mrs. McClure had left when he was only five years old, and although Sarah would never say so, she suspected Matt knew his mother only from photographs.

Matt stroked her hair. "I'm sorry if I was being pushy. I didn't mean it. I should've come right out and told you what I was thinking."

"Yes, you should have."

"I'm sorry. Really. I won't do it again."

Sarah almost retorted that she wouldn't give him the chance, that she'd be on her guard for the rest of their marriage, but he looked so remorseful that she changed her mind. "Okay," she said instead. "Let's just forget it. Besides, you're right. It would be nice if we worked at the same place."

"We might not run into each other much during the day, but at least we can have lunch together."

Sarah nodded, thinking. She'd wanted the chance to do something different with her career, and this job was certainly different. Besides, it would only be for a few months at most. It would help fill up the days and take her mind off her unsuccessful job search.

Then she remembered the quilt she'd seen on her first visit to the manor, and found another reason to take the job.

"So what do you say?" Matt asked.

"The house is gorgeous, and it's so much cooler out here, too, like you said." Sarah took Matt's hand and squeezed it. "I'm going to go back there right now and tell her I'll take the job, okay?" She turned and started back for the manor.

"Okay," Matt called after her. "See you at noon."

As she walked, Sarah decided that the situation had enough advantages to outweigh Mrs. Compson's eccentricities. She could always quit if things didn't work out. Besides, she knew the perfect way Mrs. Compson could pay her. She hurried up the back steps and knocked on the door.

Immediately, Mrs. Compson opened it. "Have you

FRIENDSHIP SAMPLER
Sampler quilts are often ideal for the beginning quilter, because she is able to experiment with many different kinds of blocks, from appliquéd to pieced. Several women contributed blocks to this 1890 Friendship sampler from the collection of Kitty Clark Cole. These quilters will not be forgotten, as they each embroidered their names onto their festively colored blocks. (Photograph © Keith Baum/BaumsAway!)

From On the Banks of Plum Creek, *1937*

By Laura Ingalls Wilder

The classic stories of Laura Ingalls Wilder have been well-loved for decades. This excerpt illustrates that just as quilts can keep you comfortable on cold mornings, so can they help you pass the time with family and friends if those frosty mornings should turn into a confining snow storm. Laura and her sister Mary are just learning to quilt, but as the girls practice, their seams get straighter and smoother, and the wintery days fly by.

Next day another blizzard came. Again that low, dark cloud rolled swiftly up from the north-west till it blotted out the sun and covered the whole sky and the wind went, howling and shrieking, whirling snow until nothing could be seen but a blur of whiteness.

Pa followed the rope to the stable and back. Ma cooked and cleaned and mended and helped Mary and Laura with their lessons. They did the dishes, made their bed, and swept the floors, kept their hands and faces clean and neatly braided their hair. They studied their books and played with Carrie and Jack. They drew pictures on their slate, and taught Carrie to make her A B C's.

Mary was still sewing nine-patch blocks. Now Laura started a bear's-track quilt. It was harder than a nine-patch, because there were bias seams, very hard to make smooth. Every seam must be exactly right before Ma would let her make another, and often Laura worked several days on one short seam.

So they were busy all day long. And all the days ran together, with blizzard after blizzard.

A QUICKER QUILT

Although some quilting traditionalists insist on hand stitching, the introduction of the sewing machine in the mid-1800s saved precious hours for quilters. The Improved Family Singer Sewing Machine, patented in 1884 by the Singer Manufacturing Company of St. Louis, Missouri, boasted one hundred different patchwork stitches, and its ad campaign promised that it "makes the finest stitch of any machine ever built."

decided?" She pursed her lips as if she expected bad news.

"I'll take the job, on one condition."

Mrs. Compson raised an eyebrow. "I already planned to feed you."

"Thank you, but that's not it."

"What, then?"

"Teach me how to quilt."

"I beg your pardon?"

"Teach me how to quilt. Teach me how to make a quilt and I'll help you with your work."

"Surely you don't mean it. There are several fine teachers in Waterford. I could give you some names."

Sarah shook her head. "No. That the deal. You teach me how to quilt, and I'll help you take inventory and prepare the manor for sale. I've seen your quilts, and—" Sarah tried to remember what Bonnie had said. "And you're in the QAS permanently. You ought to be able to teach me how to quilt."

"You mean AQS, but that's not the point. Of course I could teach you. It's not a question of my ability." The old woman eyed her as if she found her quite inscrutable, then shrugged and extended a hand. "Very well. Agreed. In addition to your wages, I'll teach you how to quilt."

Sarah pulled her hand away an instant before she would have been grasping Mrs. Compson's. "No, that's not what I meant. The lessons are my wages."

"Goodness, child, have you no bills to pay?" Mrs. Compson sighed and looked to the heavens. "Don't let these somewhat dilapidated conditions deceive you. My family may not be what it once was, but we aren't ready to accept charity quite yet."

"I didn't mean to imply that."

"Yes, yes. Of course you didn't. But I simply must insist on some sort of payment. My conscience wouldn't give me a moment's peace otherwise."

Sarah thought about it. "Okay. Something fair." She wasn't about to take advantage of someone who was obviously lonely, no matter how rude she was.

They settled on a wage, but Sarah still felt that she was receiving the best part of the bargain. When they shook on it, Mrs. Compson's eyes lit up with triumph. "I think you would have held out for more if you knew how much work there is to be done."

"I'm hoping that I'll have a real job before long."

Mrs. Compson smiled. "Forgive me if I hope not. . . ."

At four o'clock Sarah heard Mrs. Compson calling her from the bottom of the stairs. She arched her back, stretched, and wiped her brow on a clean corner of a dust cloth. There was still a lot of work to be done, but even Mrs. Compson would have to agree that Sarah had made a noticeable dent in it.

She hurried downstairs, where Mrs. Compson greeted her with an amused look. "There seems to be more dust on you than there was in the entire library."

Sarah hastily wiped her palms on her shorts and tucked in her blouse. "No, don't worry. There's plenty more dust up there for anyone who wants it."

Mrs. Compson chuckled and motioned for Sarah to follow her down the hallway. "How much did you accomplish today?"

"I took care of everything that was on the floor and finished the bookcases on the north and west walls. I closed the windows, too, in case it rains tonight. Do you want to look through anything before it's recycled?"

"Did you follow my instructions? Were you careful?"

"I think I was, but it's your stuff. I'd hate to throw out anything you might miss later. Maybe you should look through the piles just the same."

They entered the kitchen. "No need for that. Anything I ever wanted from this place isn't here for the taking." Mrs. Compson gestured to the sink. "When you've cleaned yourself up a bit, join me in the sitting room."

Sarah washed her hands and face, then hesitated in the sitting room doorway. Mrs. Compson was pulling some quilts from a cedar chest and draping them on the sofa. Open books were piled on an end table. Mrs. Compson turned and spotted her. "Well, are you coming in or aren't you? It's all right. You've been invited this time, not like that first day."

"I was kind of hoping you'd forgotten about that."

"I never forget."

Sarah figured the older woman probably never forgave, either. She entered the room and walked over to the quilts. The fabric seemed worn and faded, even

Bouquet of appliqué
This hand-stitched 1930s Flower Pot quilt seems to have a sunny disposition. Eight dozen fabric flowers have been appliquéd to the quilt top, and they are framed by a cheerful gingham border. (Minnesota Historical Society)

faintly stained in some places, but the quilting stitches and the arrangements of tiny pieces of cloth were as lovely as the newer quilts she had recently seen. Gingerly she traced the pattern of a red-and-white quilt with a fingertip. "Did you make these?"

"All of them. They're old."

"They're beautiful."

"Hmph. Young lady, if you keep saying things like that I might just have to keep you around." Mrs. Compson closed the cedar chest and spread one last quilt on the sofa. "They shouldn't be stored in there. Contact with wood can damage them. But Claudia was too scatterbrained to remember such simple things." She sighed and eased herself onto a chair beside the end table. "Not that it really matters. These quilts were made to be used, and to be used up. I thought they might at least give you some ideas, a place to start."

Claudia—she must be her sister, Sarah thought as she pulled a chair closer to Mrs. Compson's.

"The last time I taught someone to quilt—why, it must have been fifty years ago," Mrs. Compson said, as if thinking aloud. "Of course, she never truly wanted to learn. I'm sure you'll do much better."

"Oh, I really do want to learn. My grandmother quilted, but she died before I was old enough for her to teach me."

Mrs. Compson raised an eyebrow. "I learned when I was five years old." She put on her glasses and peered at one of the books. "I thought you could best learn by making a sampler. Mind you, I plan to teach you the traditional way, hand piecing and hand quilting. You shouldn't expect to finish your quilt this week or even this year."

"I know it'll take time. I don't mind."

"There are many other perfectly acceptable modern techniques that make quilting faster and easier." She indicated the sewing machine with a jerk of her head. "I use some of them myself. But for now, hand piecing will do."

Sarah looked at the small machine in disbelief.

"You can sew on that toy sewing machine?"

Matt had an expression very much like the one Mrs. Compson wore then, one he usually assumed when Sarah called an amaryllis a lily or when she called everything from mulch to peat moss dirt. "That's no toy. That model isn't manufactured anymore, but it's one of the finest sewing machines a quilter can own. You shouldn't judge things by their size, or by their age."

Chastened, Sarah changed the subject. "You said I should make a sampler?"

Mrs. Compson nodded. "How big do you want the finished quilt to be?"

"Big enough for our bed. It's queen-size."

"Then you'll need about twelve different blocks, if we use a straight setting with sashing and borders instead of setting the blocks on point. Then we'll attach wide strips of your background fabric between the blocks and your outer border so you have plenty of space to practice your hand quilting stitches." Mrs. Compson handed Sarah one of the books. "Pick twelve different blocks you'd like to try. There are more patterns in these other books. I'll help you find a good balance."

With Mrs. Compson's guidance, Sarah selected twelve blocks from the hundreds of patterns in the books. Mrs. Compson explained the difference between pieced blocks, ones that were made from seaming the block's pieces together, and appliquéd blocks, which were made by sewing figures onto background fabric. Mrs. Compson encouraged her to choose some of each style for her sampler. The time spent choosing, reconsidering, and rejecting blocks passed quickly, and before Sarah knew it, it was half past five. She had selected twelve blocks that varied in style, appearance, and difficulty, and Matt was standing in the sitting room doorway smiling at her.

"How's quilt school going?" he asked, crossing the room and giving Sarah a hug.

Sarah smiled up at him. "I'm getting my homework assignment as we speak."

Chapter 2

Our Quilting Heritage

" . . . just as the pieces of the quilt are sewn together with interlocking stitches, all people are linked together in the fabric of our world. In a way, the patchwork quilt represents all the different people in the world. We are individual in our attitudes, life-styles, and backgrounds, yet we share so much of what it means to be human."
—Teresa Gustafson, *"Love is a Blanket,"* 1990

The quilt is likely a better metaphor for our culture than the oft used "melting pot." A melting pot implies that all of its elements are stirred and combined together to form one homogenous whole. A quilt, on the other hand, consists of a wide spectrum of pieces that, while they may be stitched together to form a cohesive pattern, retain their own identity through shape and color. There are countless quilt-block variations that can be pulled from the scrapbag, but it is this variety—like the diversity of our world—that is part of the charm and appeal of the quilt.

Quilters themselves are a varied bunch, each bringing their own styles and traditions to the quilts they make. The selections in this chapter highlight just a few of the ways in which quilts have been used to create a complex and diverse North American legacy.

MOUNTAIN MIST
ABOVE: *The Stearns & Foster Company of Cincinnati, Ohio, manufactured quilting cotton under the brand name "Mountain Mist." A quilt pattern appeared on the back of each batting wrapper, making the company one of the most common ways that quilt patterns were spread across the United States and Canada. This Mountain Mist wrapper was printed in 1937.*

LIVES ON THE LINE
LEFT: *Quilts containing the stories of the hands that stitched them hang and wave in the warm summer sunshine at this Amish roadside stand in Central Michigan. (Photograph © Keith Baum/BaumsAway!)*

Quilts among the Plain People

By Rachel T. Pellman and Joanne Ranck

THERE IS SOMETHING quietly powerful about Amish quilts. The large, geometric pieces of solid-colored cotton or wool fabric that make up the order's traditional quilts comply with their conservative nature and religious commitment to a life of simplicity. Yet the boldness of color, sharp contrasts, and beauty of the quilting stitches make the Amish style one of the most revered in the world of quilting. First learned from their "English" (or non-Amish) neighbors in the mid-1800s, quilting became a mainstay in the Amish community by the 1880s and continues to be an important aspect of their way of life today.

Rachel Pellman and Joanne Ranck both grew up in the pastoral environment of Lancaster County, Pennsylvania, and are graduates of Eastern Mennonite College. Veterans of making and selling quilts, the two women collaborated to write *Quilts among the Plain People*, a close-to-the-heart look at the role quilts play in Amish and Mennonite communities. Pellman is the author of several other books, including *Amish Quilt Patterns* and *A Treasury of Mennonite Quilts*, co-written with her husband Kenneth Pellman.

■ ■ ■

Beauty among the Austere

Why do many Amish and Mennonites who are devoutly committed to a simple, austere life make beautiful quilts? Who are these people who disdain fashion and convenience, yet cultivate exquisite artistry in color and stitching?

There is no denying the fact that life in the Old Order Amish and Mennonite communities is dramatically disciplined. Both large and small matters in life are governed by what the brotherhood believes. One's dress, mode of transportation, vocation and entertainment are affected by commonly held convictions and strong social pressures within the group. But these boundaries have distinct advantages. There is freedom in knowing limits and inside these limits is great room to grow.

Appreciation for beauty is not lost when life is austere. Rather, it seems intensified. It becomes more vivid in minute details. Flower beds and gardens are tended with love and care. There is delight in the breakthrough of a bean sprout not only because of the food it eventually brings but for the joy of seeing a full straight row of new green shoots. Flower beds bring new delight every year with the marvels of bright colors. Beauty in nature is admired heartily.

"Quilts for Sale"
Artist Diane Phalen often says, "I quilt with my paintbrush." A native of Pennsylvania who now makes her home in Banks, Oregon, Phalen is best known for her collection of quilt watercolors. She focuses much of her work on Amish country life— here, a household with quilts hanging on the front fence broadcasts the well-respected Amish rule "No Sunday Sales." (Artwork © Diane Phalen)

Among these people personal beauty is handled more gingerly. There is no room for individual pride within the fellowship. Regulations on dress and lifestyle are in part to squelch temptations toward vanity. But the line here is delicate. In work, a job well done is imperative, yet pride in that job is not tolerated. Doing it well is only doing what is expected. But there are exceptions, and quilting may be one of them. Here is an avenue where a woman may show off her abilities unashamedly. In a community where restraint inhibits public displays of emotion and physical contact, a quilt shows love much the same way a favorite food is carefully prepared as a display of affection.

Amish Quilts From Long Ago

If in defining Amish Quilts one speaks of quilts made by the Amish, they are as abundant today as ever before. Amish women are accomplished artisans in the realm of quiltmaking. Although their style of life and manner of dress is held within strong boundaries, their quilts show great freedom and bright splashes of color.

Amish women today make quilts in a wide variety of patterns. In fact, there is little distinction between those quilts made by Amish and those made by Mennonites or other quilters. Many buy fabrics especially for quiltmaking and so carefully coordinate calicoes and solid color fabrics into a well blended whole.

There is another definition of Amish Quilts; those that belong to the era of "what has been." These are the quilts with characteristics making them distinctly different from their contemporaries. The Amish quilts made in the 19th century and up to 1940 had an identity of their own. They were quilts using only the solid colors of Amish clothing in intriguing and unusual ways. The quilting was abundant and exquisite, showing off beautifully in the characteristically wide solid borders. Quilting thread was often black and the effect on the dark fabrics was a soft sculptured design.

The charm of these earlier quilts is difficult to duplicate. The patterns are often copied but the subtle colors of the natural fibers and the painstaking, expert workmanship are lost to later generations. They stand apart today as a statement of a people with firm roots and strong identity. The colors and patterns are bold and yet there is a restraint and delicate balance maintained with the skilled use of designs held within definite borders. Three of the most commonly recognized Amish patterns are Sunshine and Shadow, Diamond in Square, and Bars.

Sunshine and Shadow

There is something striking, almost shocking about this quilt. Perhaps it is because it is associated with the Old Order Amish whose quiet, subdued manner seems to defy such a statement. Sunshine and Shadow gets its name from the light and dark effect created by the blending and juxtaposition of a large variety of bold solid colors. It is a dramatic quilt but its vibrance is contained inside a strong, solid border.

Sunshine and Shadow is a simple quilt. It is small squares sewn together to form a series of brightly colored expanding squares. Or the squares may be tipped on their sides forming a pattern of concentric diamonds. Its uniqueness is in its use of only solid colors put together in a way that might at first seem odd but on second glance is strangely beautiful.

Sunshine and Shadow is an old favorite with Amish quiltmakers. Perhaps the first quilt happened merely by accident—the scraps from the bright solid colors of Amish clothing being used in a functional way. At any rate, its effect was so gripping, so surprising in its boldness that it is a pattern much in demand outside Amish circles even today. Sadly enough, it is almost impossible to recreate the original look. The natural fibers of cotton and wool colored with dyes from nature have a warmth and subtlety not to be achieved in the new synthetics. The colors are blues, maroons, pinks, deep greens, purple, mauves and black—the shades used in Amish shirts and dresses.

The arrangement of the squares is not necessarily Amish. Another quilt, also using small squares in the same arrangement but with printed fabrics would be called Trip Around the World. The Trip Around the World quilt may or may not have a border while the Sunshine and Shadow has a distinctively wide border. It is often elaborately quilted with generous feathers. This quilting represents the work of an experienced artisan. The small continuous curves of the feathers make quilting much more difficult than straight lines or larger patterns.

QUILT AUCTION
Small, contrasting squares produce the dramatic effect of the Sunshine and Shadow pattern. The bids for this quilt, which is being sold at an Amish auction, will likely total hundreds of dollars. (Photograph © Jerry Irwin)

Diamond in Square

Another Amish quilt using geometric shapes is the Diamond in Square or Center Diamond pattern. This is one large solid color diamond surrounded by a double border—one narrow and one wide. This quilt traditionally uses only three or four colors and they are again colors of Amish clothing—deep, vibrant solids. It is difficult to decide what is more outstanding about this quilt—the bold pattern or the quilting. It is usually quilted in black with the small tight stitches creating a beautiful pattern that softens the sharp lines. Typical quilting patterns would be a circular feather filled with diamonds or a star or tulips. On older quilts grapes and grape leaves may have been used on the narrow border. The Center Diamond quilt is vibrant when its quilting is done masterfully.

Bars

A third example of a traditional Amish design is Bars. Here again the pattern is composed of large pieces of fabric, arranged to form large vertical bars usually in two different solid colors surrounded by a double border. The quilting in the center of the quilt is often less elaborate than in the Center Diamond pattern. Bars may be covered with only small quilted diamonds (cross-hatching) in keeping with the strong straight lines already established. The border however creates a challenge for any avid quilter with an abundance of feathers, cables, or other delicately stitched patterns.

These quilts, although old and traditional, are making a comeback as wallhangings. They appear modern in their boldness both in design and color. The irony of this situation is that the Amish themselves would probably never use them as such.

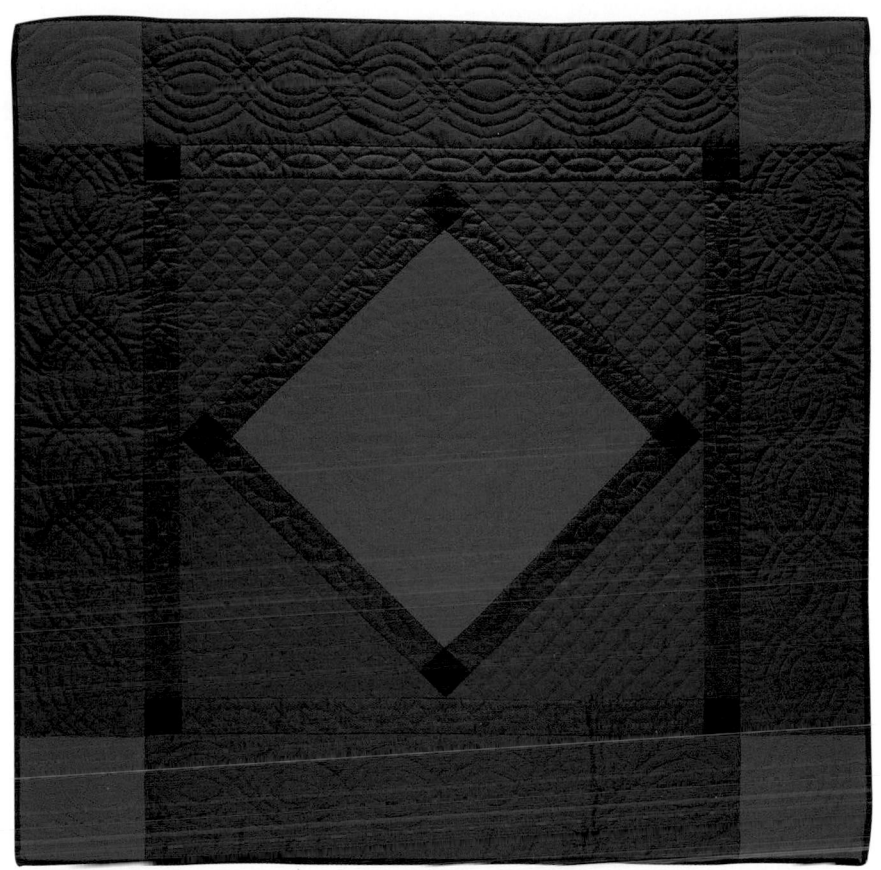

DIAMOND IN THE SQUARE
Also known as the Diamond Center pattern, this quilt is an Amish favorite. It is reminiscent of the Medallion quilts that were popular in North America in the first half of the nineteenth century. The quilt pictured here, from Sylvia Petersheim Quilts & Crafts, illustrates that the simplicity of large, solid-colored fabric pieces allow the detailed quilting stitches to stand out beautifully. (Photograph © Keith Baum/BaumsAway!)

AMISH BARS
Quilts were made from leftover scraps when possible, but for patterns that used large expanses of fabric, such as the Bars design, bolts of fabric were bought especially for them. This striking Bars quilt comes from Lovina's Stitchery in Strasburg, Pennsylvania. (Photograph © Keith Baum/ BaumsAway!)

Quilting Folklore

"At your quilting, maids, don't tarry.
Quilt quick if you would marry.
A maid who is quiltless at twenty-one,
Never shall greet her bridal sun."
—Traditional verse

The Amish believe that a flaw should purposely be included in each quilt, because only God is perfect. This is only one of a multitude of quilting superstitions that are woven into the lore of quilters everywhere. A sampling of some of the more commonly heard customs, wisdoms, and warnings follow.

- If a young girl slept under a new quilt, she would dream of the boy she was going to marry.

- Any boy who slept under a Wandering Foot quilt pattern would eventually leave home and begin a life of aimless wandering. Mothers and wives solved this problem by simply renaming the pattern "Turkey Tracks."

- Unmarried girls and boys were to put a cat in the middle of a new quilt. They then would hold the edges of the quilt and toss the cat into the air. Whoever was closest to the disgruntled and disoriented cat when it landed would be the next to marry.

- A heart pattern used in any quilt but a bride's quilt was considered unlucky and could cause an engagement to be broken.

- A young woman should have twelve quilts by the time she married to ensure a blissful life.

A young Amish girl works intently on a Double Wedding Ring design, as sunlight streams through the window and daydreams of a future husband. The Double Wedding Ring quilt was traditionally made in preparation for a wedding day, as its intertwined and unbroken circles poignantly symbolize the bond of marriage. (Photograph © Jerry Irwin)

Hidden in Plain View

By Jacqueline L. Tobin and Raymond G. Dobard, Ph.D.

JACQUELINE TOBIN, THE author of *Hidden in Plain View* and *The Tao Women*, is a collector and teller of women's stories. When she ventured from her home in Denver, Colorado, to Charleston, South Carolina, and met quilter Ozella McDaniel Williams, Tobin stumbled upon a fascinating piece of unwritten quilting history: According to Ozella, quilts had been used by African American slaves as a code to help them plan the course of their escape on the Underground Railroad. The innocent quilt being aired out on the clothesline was certainly not readable to slave owners, but to slaves who had learned the code and were ready to begin their journey to freedom, these quilts served as maps of hope.

Tobin teamed up with Raymond Dobard, an art history professor at Howard University and a nationally known African American quilter living in Washington, D.C., to explore what they dubbed "Ozella's Underground Railroad Quilt Code." The following selection from *Hidden in Plain View* details Tobin's first meeting with Ozella and the heart of her spellbinding story.

■ ■ ■

In 1994 I traveled to Charleston, South Carolina, to learn more about the sweet-grass baskets unique to this area and to hear the stories of the African American craftswomen who make them. Charleston is rich in history. A port city, where the Ashley River meets the Cooper to form (as locals like to say) the beginnings of the Atlantic Ocean, Charleston today is a place whose buildings and culture reflect the combined and separate histories of American and African American peoples. It is unique as the location where black slaves first set foot on American soil and once outnumbered the white population four to one.

A walk through the historic district of Charleston is like a walk through the corridors of American Southern history. Here, one is confronted by all the hustle and bustle of the retentions and re-creations of a bygone era. At the heart of historic Charleston is an imposing brick enclosure with open sides, known as the Old Marketplace. It looks very much as it did over one hundred years ago, as it still defines the length of the district. As it was in years gone by, the Marketplace is still the center of commerce for the area. Under the roof of the structure, long wooden tables, laid end-to-end, go on for blocks to create two narrow avenues for selling wares. As early as 1841 it was a marketplace for fresh vegetables, fish, meats, and other goods brought to Charleston from the surrounding farms and plantations and other coastal ports and faraway lands; it is still

TUMBLING BLOCKS
This quilt from 1898 illustrates that a pattern can be viewed in various ways. The diamond-shaped pieces in the design create an optical illusion of sorts, as they appear to build on each other to create stacks of blocks. Looking closely at the quilt reveals a star pattern as well. (Minnesota Historical Society)

IMPROVISATION

Quilt historians theorize that there are several features that may characterize an African American quilt, including vertical strips, bright colors, large designs, asymmetrical or multiple patterns, and improvisational elements. This Blue Jean Pockets quilt was made in 1990 by Essie Lee Robinson of Detroit, Michigan. (Courtesy of Michigan State University Museum)

a vendor's market, but with stark contrasts between the old and the new. African American women sit by pails of sweet grass and weave baskets much as their African ancestors did over a hundred years ago. But these craftswomen, many of them descendants of slaves, are now surrounded by merchants of flea market trinkets, Southern memorabilia, and newer, cheaper baskets from China and Thailand.

The smell of the daily ocean catch or freshly slaughtered meats is no longer the predominant early morning smell of the Marketplace. Today the aroma of freshly baked cookies and newly ground coffee beans from the gourmet shops surrounding the area compete for attention. Certain sounds can still be heard; the din of tourists and locals alike crowding the streets and trying to avoid the horses, their hooves providing the percussive rhythm for this city as they clop loudly over original cobblestone streets. Carriages are drawn around the district, past the Custom House and on toward the Battery, where decorative wrought-iron fences accentuate the largess of old historic homes. Taverns and brothels have given way to fern bars and upscale hotels touting Southern hospitality and cui-

sine. Newly restored, on a lesser traveled street, is the original slave mart, now a historical museum, whose presence jars us into remembering a less civil piece of the history of this Southern port city.

As I walked the aisles of the Marketplace, I found myself standing in front of a stall lined with quilts of all sizes, colors, and patterns. I was drawn in by these piles of quilts, as long-forgotten memories of my grandmother's quilt box, filled with her handmade quilts, were brought to mind. Before I could do much looking or reminiscing, an elderly African American woman, dressed in brightly colored, geometrically patterned African garb, slowly walked up to me from the back of the stall. She motioned me to follow her to the back, where an old metal folding chair sat surrounded by more quilts. "Look," she said. She chose one of the quilts from the pile, unrolled it, and while pointing to it said, "Did you know that quilts were used by slaves to communicate on the Underground Railroad?" The old quilter continued to speak but I could not hear her clearly in the midst of the noise of the Marketplace around us. I wasn't sure why she was telling me, a complete stranger, this unusual story. I

SPRING CLEANING
After a long winter of use, quilts are often hung outside to air out and absorb the fresh, clean scent of spring. (Photograph © Kent and Donna Dannen)

listened politely for a short while. When I didn't ask any questions, she stopped talking. I purchased a beautiful, hand-tied quilt and left with her flyer advertising "historic Charleston Marketplace" quilts.

I returned home with my quilt and memories of Charleston. I hung my quilt and laid my memories aside. I didn't think too much about my conversation with this quilter until several months later when I came across her flyer again. I remembered the story she had started to tell me and I wondered about it. I had never heard such a story or read about it in any books. Was there more to the story? The flyer listed the quilter's name and phone number. I decided to call Mrs. Ozella McDaniel Williams and see if she would be willing to tell me more. When she answered the phone, I reminded her of who I was and asked if I might hear more about how quilts were used on the Underground Railroad. She told me curtly to call back the next evening, which I did. At that time she said, "I can't speak to you about this right now." When I tried pressing her, she laughed quietly and whispered into the phone, "Don't worry, you'll get the story when you are ready." And then she hung up.

Ozella had now added an element of intrigue to the already fascinating story. I was hooked. What did she mean by "you'll get the story when you're ready"? I felt I had to explore the story further. If she wouldn't talk, perhaps others would. I began to contact every African American quilter and quilt scholar I could find. I traveled down the Mississippi from St. Louis to New Orleans, stopping to visit quilters and scholars. I toured plantations and slave quarters, looking for clues. Before long, I was speaking to a fairly close-knit circle of people that included art historians, African American quilters, African textile experts, and folklorists. Most of them had heard that quilts had been used as a means of secret communication on the Underground Railroad, but none were exactly sure how. Some referenced particular quilt patterns, some mentioned the stitching, and others cited specific colors. I was not able to find any slave quilts that could verify these

THE CODE OF THE QUILT
Slaves in the antebellum South may have been able to read the Underground Railroad Quilt Code in various common quilt patterns. The Log Cabin quilt, like the Barn Raising variation pictured here from Sylvia Petersheim Quilts & Crafts, is thought to have directed escaping slaves to a safe haven. (Photograph © Keith Baum/BaumsAway!)

stories. Most quilt scholars agreed that few slave quilts had survived the constant strain of excessive use, the poor quality of fabric they had probably been sewn from, and the continual washing in harsh lye soap that would eventually cause them to disintegrate.

As a white person conducting research into African American scholarship, I was hesitant at times to continue. Some people were reluctant to share family stories with me. At one point I suggested that Dr. Raymond Dobard, one of the scholars I was conversing with, continue my research by contacting Ozella himself. I was hoping that she would speak more freely to another African American. Raymond, an art history professor at Howard University, a renowned quilter, and a known expert on African American quilts as they relate to the Underground Railroad, seemed to me to be the perfect person to pursue this research with Ozella. However, when I made my suggestion, Raymond insisted that I was the one with whom Ozella felt comfortable telling the story initially and thus should be the one to pursue it. He told me to be patient and that I would indeed get the story when I was ready. With his encouragement I continued my research.

Three years after first hearing the story, I had come full circle with my research, but there were still missing pieces. I could add nothing new to the information that was already out there. Still lacking was an elaboration of the story connecting quilts and the Underground Railroad. I was hoping for a final link connecting all the quilt stories with details. My intuition told me that Ozella knew more than what she'd already told me. The only way to find out would be to return to Charleston and see if she would speak to me again.

Without contacting her first, I arranged a return visit to Charleston. If Ozella was reluctant to speak, I didn't want to give her any time to think about it and turn me down without my ability to plead my case in person. Besides, I had done my homework, and maybe, I thought, I was now "ready" to receive the story in full. Armed with information and questions, I felt the time was right.

Upon my arrival, I took a carriage tour around the historic Charleston district. I wanted to immerse myself once again in the flavor of the Old South before attempting to talk with Ozella. As the carriage passed the Marketplace, I turned to took, my eyes straining to recognize my quilter friend's face. I recognized her immediately, sitting in the same location, amidst her tables of quilts, just as I had seen her three years prior. Today she was dressed all in white. She had on white slacks and a white blouse decorated with a huge lavender flower hand-painted on the front. She wore a large straw hat with a white band that had the same lavender flower painted on it as well.

I completed my carriage ride and walked slowly down the aisles of the Marketplace. I was nervous about meeting her again. Would she remember me? I wondered. What if I had come this far and she still wouldn't speak to me? Or, worse yet, what if she really didn't know anything more than she had already told me? With notebook in hand I took a deep breath and hesitantly approached her. Her back was turned to me as she stood quietly arranging her quilts. I cleared my throat to get her attention. When she turned, I tried to hand her my business card and started to explain who I was and why I was there. With a wave of her hand, brushing my card away, she interrupted me and said, "I don't care who you is. You is people and that is all that matters. Bring over some of those quilts and make a seat for yourself beside me. Get yourself comfortable."

I hesitated, but only briefly. If she was ready to talk, I was ready to listen. I was concerned about sitting on her handmade works of art, but she didn't seem to care. She positioned herself on the metal folding chair, moving quilts to either side of her and around her. I chose several rolled quilts and brought them over in front of her. After placing them on the ground, I sat down in front of her. From this position I was looking directly up into Ozella's face. She pulled her folding chair even closer to me. I became aware that she was now physically creating a space around us, obviously meant only for her and me. After seating herself on the folding chair she leaned down toward me, one hand resting on her knee, her index finger pointing to my notepad. She pushed her straw hat farther back on her head and with her other hand she directed me, "Write this down."

From the moment she said those words until she finished speaking about three hours later, time stood still. The normal chaos of Saturday morning at the Marketplace ceased to exist for us. Nothing and no one entered this space to disturb us. It was as if what she was going to say was for my ears only and that this

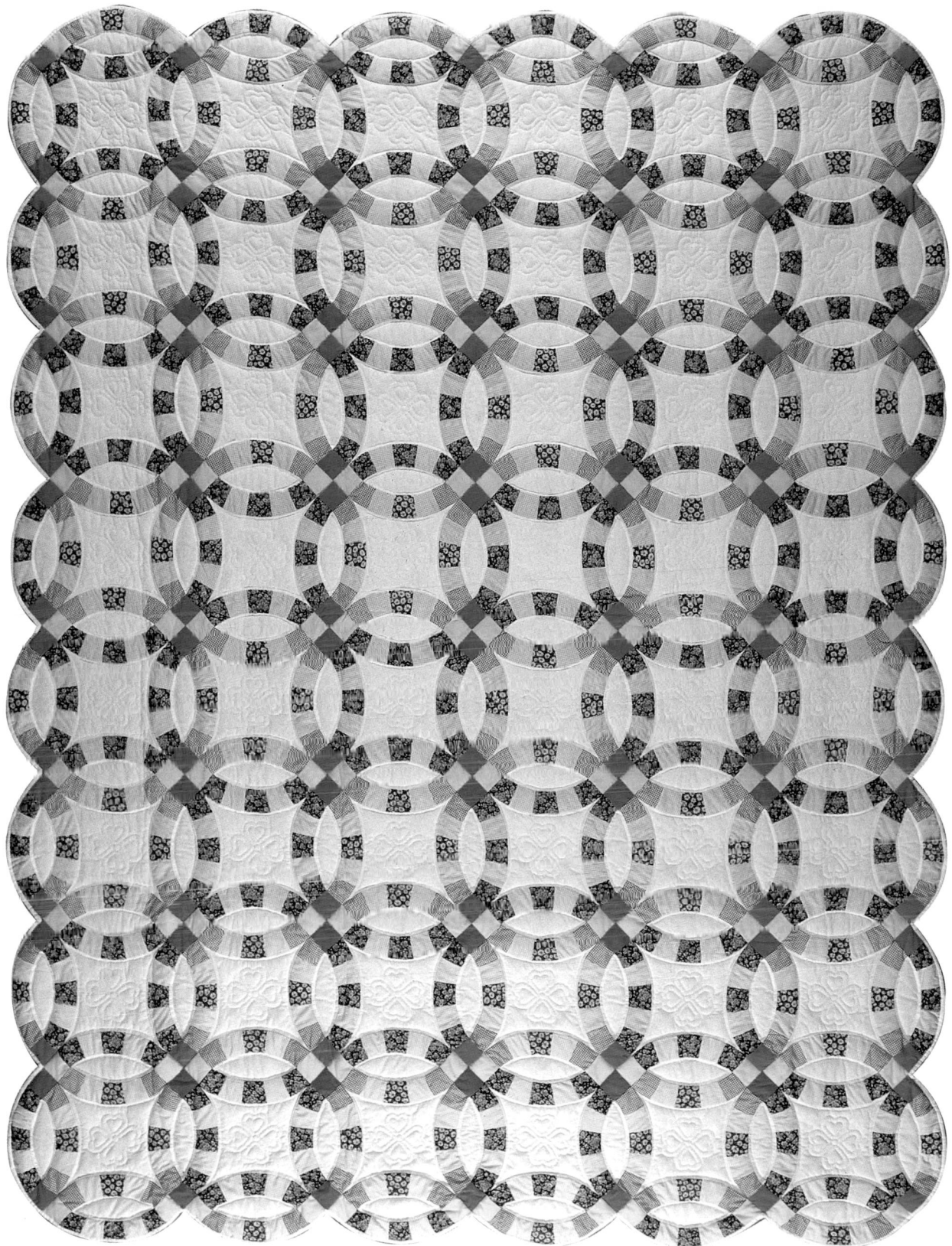

DOUBLE WEDDING RING
To slaves escaping on the Underground Railroad, the Double Wedding Ring design may have symbolized taking off their chains and breaking from the bonds of slavery. This beautiful example from Sylvia Petersheim Quilts & Crafts features the notable pattern. (Photograph © Keith Baum/BaumsAway!)

Ozella's Underground Railroad Quilt Code

■ ■ ■

There are *five square knots* on the quilt every *two inches apart*.
They escaped on the *fifth knot* on the *tenth pattern* and went to Ontario, Canada.

The **monkey wrench** 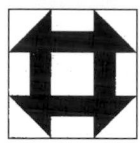 turns the **wagon wheel**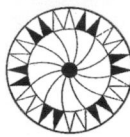

toward Canada on a **bear's paw**  trail to the **crossroads**.

Once they got to the **crossroads** they dug a **log cabin** 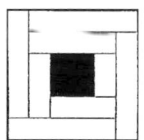 on the ground.

Shoofly 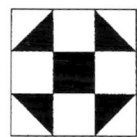 told them to dress up in cotton and satin **bow ties**

and go to the cathedral church, get married and exchange **double wedding rings**.

Flying geese  stay on the **drunkard's path**

and follow the **stars**.

time and space had been set aside for me to hear it. I felt that fate was honoring this moment. With a far-away look in her eyes, reciting something from memory, Ozella instructed me on what to write, stopping now and then only to ask me to read it back to her.

It took all my journalistic energies to focus on writing the words she spoke and to not get lost in the art of her telling. I was the student; she was the teacher. I was the transcriber; she the storyteller. At that moment, I knew that I was one of only a trusted few people who, down through history, had been told to listen carefully and remember the words she was speaking. Sitting beside this elderly black woman, surrounded in a sea of her handiwork, I felt that she was inviting me to share in her family stories and memories and become a part of an oral tradition that had allowed her culture to survive. I was no longer the journalist in search of a story. My role was to be much different. I felt that Ozella had very purposefully created an atmosphere where I was to receive this information. Surrounding us were only the sounds of her ancestors, family members like her mother and grandmother before her, passing words of information from one woman to another for safekeeping. During this time, I was aware of nothing but her voice and her message and the awesome responsibility she was giving me to write the story down. Seated at the feet of an older woman, I was conscious that we were taking part in a time-honored women's ritual of passing on wisdom from one generation to another. I was aware that we were bridging not only a gap of generations but also one of race. We were transcending age, stereotypes, and boundaries.

Because of its imagery, Ozella's Underground Railroad Quilt Code lends itself to conjecture. Exactly how the code was used, we do not know. However, Ozella's words and our research enable us to theorize the following. The quilt patterns listed in the code were intended as mnemonic devices. They were used to aid the slaves in memorizing directives before leaving the plantation. The names of quilt patterns function as metaphors in the code; in other words, the patterns represent certain meanings.

When Ozella first revealed the code to Jacki, she instructed her to write down the numbers one through ten. She then listed nine patterns and one phrase: Monkey Wrench, Wagon Wheel, Log Cabin, Shoofly,

Bow Ties, Cathedral Church, Double Wedding Rings, Flying Geese, Drunkard's Path, and Tumbling Boxes. Then Ozella recited the code. However, the code she recited also included the following quilt pattern names: Bear's Paw, Crossroads, and Stars (North Star).

Why were they excluded from the original list? We can explain.

According to Ozella, there were ten quilts used to direct the slaves to take particular actions. Each quilt featured one of the ten patterns. The ten quilts were placed one at a time on a fence. Since it was common for quilts to be aired out frequently, the master and mistress would not be suspicious when seeing the quilts displayed in this fashion. This way, the slaves could nonverbally alert those who were escaping. Only one quilt would appear at any one time. Each quilt signaled a specific action for a slave to take at the particular time that the quilt was on view. Ozella explained that when the Monkey Wrench quilt pattern was displayed, the slaves were to gather all the tools they might need on the journey to freedom. The second quilt placed on the fence was the Wagon Wheel pattern, which signaled the slaves to pack all the things that would go in a wagon or that would be used in transit. When the quilt with the Tumbling Boxes pattern appeared, the slaves knew it was time to escape. How long each quilt remained on the fence before being replaced is not known. Ozella suspected that a quilt would remain up until all who were planning to escape had completed the signaled task. The code had dual meaning: first to signal slaves to prepare to escape and second to give clues and indicate directions on the journey.

We strongly believe that in order to memorize the whole code, a sampler quilt was used. The sampler quilt would include all of the patterns arranged in the order of the code. Traditionally the sampler quilt was used to teach pattern piecing. Think of it as a book of fabric patterns. If the mistress or anyone saw the griot conducting a class on patterns, praise for industrious behavior would be the outcome. No one would suspect what was really taking place.

Together, the quilt patterns as metaphors and as signs instructed the escaping slaves on how to prepare for escape, what to do on the journey, and where to go. The quilt patterns worked in conjunction with spirituals and topographical stitching to create a map in the mind of those escaping.

Quilts and the Hopi Baby-Naming Ceremony

By Marlene Sekaquaptewa and Carolyn O'Bagy Davis

ALTHOUGH QUILTING WAS passed to Native Americans by European immigrants, Native tribes have made the craft their own. Many quilting techniques were originally learned through formal instruction and quilting bees organized by Christian missions. Today, it is evident that the quilts made in Native American communities have several influences, including Euro-American, African American, and Hispanic American. The Native American quilt is truly a patchwork of the different cultures that compose North America.

Quilts now play a part in many Native American celebrations and rituals. In this essay, which first appeared in *To Honor and Comfort: Native Quilting Traditions*, Marlene Sekaquaptewa of the Hopi tribe and Carolyn O'Bagy Davis describe how the quilt is incorporated into the lives of the Hopi.

■ ■ ■

Today, second- and third-generation quilters live in every village on the Hopi mesas. Quilting bees are a weekly activity among the women at the mission churches and community centers, and quilts are often displayed at local village craft shows. Not surprisingly, quilts have become part of Hopi life and ceremony. Quilts are often the favored gift to celebrate a wedding or birthday. When a daughter or son leaves home to attend school or work off the reservation, he or she carries a quilt as a remembrance of home and family. Hopi women use quilts to chronicle important events within their family and community, just as quilters across the country instinctively stitch a quilt to mark a noteworthy occasion and give a tangible token of their regard and affection.

Quilts have also been integrated into some beautiful Hopi ceremonies, most notably the baby-naming ceremony. When a Hopi baby is born, infant and mother are secluded inside their home for twenty days. Traditionally, the house was kept dark during this time with a blanket draped in front of the door and coverings hung over the windows. At harvesttime or well before the birth of the baby, two perfect ears of white corn would be selected and set aside. These mother ears will be placed next to the baby in the bassinet or cradle and will stay near the infant until the naming ceremony takes place. Later, they will be saved as a spiritual memento of the child's birth.

Early every morning, the paternal grandmother comes to the new mother's home to care for the mother and child. Every fifth day there is a ritual hair washing and bathing with yucca soap. The new mother observes a ritual fast for twenty days, eating no meat, animal fat, or salt. A special dish of whole cobs of corn cooked in water mixed with cedar leaves is always available to be offered to close friends who come to visit.

Before dawn on the twentieth morning, the infant's paternal grandmother and female relatives gather at the home for a ritual washing and blessing of the baby. Each woman brings a small jar of water that is used to wash the mother's hair. Next, fresh water is poured into the basin to symbolically bathe the mother. Then the baby is bathed in clean water, with all of the women ritually helping. After the baby is dressed, his or her face is rubbed with white cornmeal. The paternal grandmother then sits with the baby on her lap and wraps the child with a quilt that she has purchased or stitched for her new grandchild. After wrapping the baby with the quilt, she strokes its breast with the mother ears of corn and repeats a blessing. She says a prayer for the child to live a long life in good health and strength, and with her blessing she offers a clan-associated name to the child.

After the grandmother's blessing, family and friends are invited to offer a blessing and give a name to the baby. A gift of a quilt accompanies the offered name, and sometimes, if there are a lot of family and friends participating, the baby almost disappears under a mountain of quilts in this warm and endearing celebration. In earlier times, the child's father or godfather wove a special blanket for the child and the child received only one wrapping. Older women recall that as quilting became more prevalent in the Hopi villages, a quilt was substituted for, and by the early 1900s had replaced, the handwoven blanket. By the 1930s, accounts of the naming ceremony show multiple gifts of quilts as com-

NAVAJO QUILT
Although Native Americans learned the art of quiltmaking from other cultures, they soon began to incorporate bold colors and designs that made them distinctly their own. Choctaw tribe members Vera and Ruth Tyler of Clifton, Louisiana, looked to Navajo rug patterns when creating this king-size quilt in 1996. (Courtesy of Michigan State University Museum)

mon practice. Today, it is not uncommon for a baby to be given eight or ten clan names and quilts.

After the blessings and the gifts, the baby is taken by the mother and the paternal grandmother to the eastern edge of the village to greet the morning sun. The child is presented and prayers are said to *Taawa* (the Father-Sun) to ensure the child's growth in good health under his watchful presence. The mother and grandmother repeat the names given to the child, and, after the last blessing, mother, grandmother, and child return home for a ritual feast of special foods.

For this meal, the father's family butchers a sheep that is cubed and cooked in a stew with hominy. The mother's family contributes great quantities of *piki* bread, a wafer-thin bread made of blue cornmeal, and *pikami*, a traditional corn pudding. This pudding, an essential part of the feast, is made of white cornmeal ground to a fine powder. Sprouted wheat that has been dried and ground is stirred in with a greasewood stirring stick, then sugar and boiling water are added. The pudding is poured into a large metal container and put in an underground oven to bake overnight. Huge quantities of pikami are prepared to feed the anticipated crowd of friends, family, and other villagers.

After the blessings a crier stands on a rooftop welcoming everyone in the village to the home to eat. The oldest male in the home takes a small bit of food outside and ritually offers it to the spiritual leaders and ancestors, and more prayers are given asking for guidance in the life of the new infant and the eventual blessing of more children for the family. Before the meal begins a pinch of corn pudding is dipped into the hominy stew and then placed in the honored baby's mouth, and the grandmother says, "This is the food we eat." Then the other family and guests are served. When the paternal relatives have eaten and are ready to leave, the mother and maternal relatives present them with gifts of piki and pastries, a sort of ritual payment for giving a name. Any other leftover foods are given to the paternal mother-in-law.

Many Hopi women, especially the older ones, feel strongly that observing the baby-naming ceremony is

QUILT OF HONOR
A Native American man proudly wears a hand-stitched quilt around his shoulders. Quilts have been used in Native American communities not only as bedcovers, but also as hammocks, cradles, gifts on special occasions, fundraising items, and family albums. (Glenbow Archives, Calgary, Canada, NA-667-566)

HOPI NINE-PATCH
This quilt is made with patches that were given to Hopi missions by women of the White Cross. It was pieced and tied in 1996 by Pearl Nuvangyaoma of Second Mesa, Arizona. (Courtesy of Michigan State University Museum)

one of the most important things that can be done for Hopi society. Names are very important among the Hopi people; a name gives an identity. Names given at the naming ceremony always have a clan association, and the child will generally become known by one of the names offered. At other times in a Hopi's life other names may be given, all very important to the identity of the individual. The naming ceremony honors a new life and incorporates that young one into the family, but on a larger scale the ceremony also reaffirms the membership and responsibility of each individual within the Hopi community. With its emphasis on family responsibilities, the blessings, and consumption of special foods, all made with the life-giving corn, the baby-naming ceremony is endowed with parallels that mirror the larger role of the individual within Hopi culture. Hopi belief does not distinguish between

the temporal and the spiritual world. The name given to a Hopi enters the child into an already established pattern; the clan system brings him into that life an prepares him to be known as a Hopi when he goes into the next world.

It is of no small consequence that the quilt is an integral part of the ritual. A gift of a quilt is a literal gift of warmth, as well as a symbolic blessing. Long after the naming ceremony, a quilt endures as a tangible piece of love and a link to the extended family members who will always be a part of the child's life. Children are treasured by the Hopi people, and on any trip to the Hopi mesas a visitor will see beautiful Hopi babies wrapped in handmade quilts, gifts from this important ritual that wrap them within the circle of an ancient and tightly integrated community.

MISSION WORK

Christian denominational missions played a substantial role in bringing quiltmaking and other needlework to Native American communities. Quilting bees set up by missions not only provided formal instruction but also brought the women of the tribe together—Sioux women, for example would typically quilt alone unless a bee was organized. In this photograph from 1897, a finished quilt hangs behind four women making lace at the Redwood Mission in Morton, Minnesota. (Photograph by E. A. Bromley, Minnesota Historical Society)

SHADES OF SIGNIFICANCE

Lula Red Cloud, a Lakota Sioux quiltmaker from the Pine Ridge Reservation in South Dakota, uses color to convey a specific meaning. In the 1996 Morning Star quilt pictured here, her vibrant colors represent the sun, earth, and sky. (Courtesy of Michigan State University Museum)

CHAPTER 3

Comfort & Joy

"What with rearin' a family, and tendin' to a home, and all my chores—that quilt was a long time in the frame. The story of my life is pieced into it. All my joys and all my sorrows."
—Quilter from Lincoln County, West Virginia,
The Mountain Artisans Quilting Book, 1973

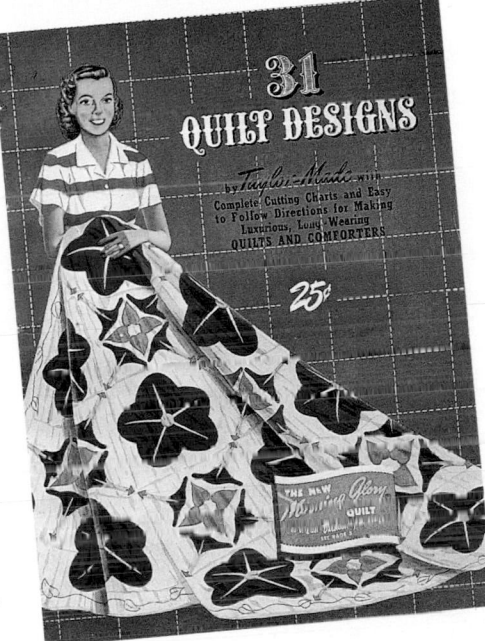

There are many reasons to make a patchwork quilt. Necessity was the most common instigator in the early days of quiltmaking—when long, uncut bolts of fabric were a luxury, but thick winter blankets were still needed. Out of this necessity, however, a mode of self-expression was born. Women found a creative outlet in quiltmaking that had previously been absent in their lives. Lively color combinations and intricate patterns brought a new joy and sense of pride to this aspect of their everyday household work.

Today, women and men make quilts for different reasons. Necessity and function can certainly still play a role, as quilts in this day and age are just as warm and comforting as they were in the 1800s, but often the feeling of happiness and satisfaction that comes with creating something beautiful is the most important reward.

The stories in this chapter tell of quiltmakers past and present who glean both comfort and joy from the completion of each lovingly stitched quilt.

IDEAS FOR SALE
ABOVE: *The woman on this vintage quilt designs booklet seems thrilled with her newly-finished Morning Glory quilt. For only twenty-five cents, any ambitious quilter could buy an identical pattern.*

HARMONY IN THE HOME
LEFT: *Two women pause patiently in their quiltmaking to listen to a guitar serenade. But though the song may be sweet, it appears that they would rather be quilting. The sewing machine, like the treadle model pictured in this 1890s hand-colored photograph, was a wonderful, time-saving innovation, making patchwork even more enjoyable. (The Fred Hultstrand History in Pictures Collection, NDIRS-NDSU, Fargo)*

The Bedquilt

By *Dorothy Canfield Fisher*

DOROTHY CANFIELD FISHER was an acute observer of small-town American life. Born in Lawrence, Kansas, Fisher received a Ph.D. in Romance languages from Columbia University. She inherited her great-grandfather's farm in Arlington, Vermont, in 1907, and used the people and places of Arlington as models for the yarns she spun about everyday folk, including the stories in *Hillsboro People* and *The Bent Twig*.

"The Bedquilt" is one of Dorothy Canfield Fisher's most humorous and touching pieces. In it, a selfless old woman pours her heart and soul, as well as innumerable hours, into piecing and quilting a remarkable one-of-a-kind masterpiece. What results is not only a quilt of unsurpassed beauty, but a measure of well-deserved recognition and self-satisfaction.

■ ■ ■

HUMBLE PRIZEWINNER
This wise-looking woman holds her quilting masterpiece, which took first prize at the Minnesota State Fair in 1926. (Photograph by Paul Hamilton, Minnesota Historical Society)

Of all the Elwell family Aunt Mehetabel was certainly the most unimportant member. It was in the old-time New England days, when an unmarried woman was an old maid at twenty, at forty was everyone's servant, and at sixty had gone through so much discipline that she could need no more in the next world. Aunt Mehetabel was sixty-eight.

She had never for a moment known the pleasure of being important to anyone. Not that she was useless in her brother's family; she was expected, as a matter of course, to take upon herself the most tedious and uninteresting part of the household labors. On Mondays she accepted as her share the washing of the men's shirts, heavy with sweat and stiff with dirt from the fields and from their own hardworking bodies. Tuesdays she never dreamed of being allowed to iron anything pretty or even interesting, like the baby's white dresses or the fancy aprons of her young lady nieces. She stood all day pressing out a monotonous succession of dish-cloths and towels and sheets.

In preserving-time she was allowed to have none of the pleasant responsibility of deciding when the fruit had cooked long enough, nor did she share in the little excitement of pouring the sweet-smelling stuff into the stone jars. She sat in a corner with the children and stoned cherries incessantly, or hulled strawberries until her fingers were dyed red.

The Elwells were not consciously unkind to their aunt, they were even in a vague way fond of her; but she was so insignificant a figure in their lives that she was almost invisible to them. Aunt Mehetabel did not resent this treatment; she took it quite as unconsciously as they gave it. It was to be expected when one was an old-maid dependent in a busy family. She gathered what crumbs of comfort she could from their occasional careless kindnesses and tried to hide the hurt which even yet pierced her at her brother's rough joking. In the winter when they all sat before the big hearth, roasted apples, drank mulled cider, and teased the girls about their beaux and the boys about their sweethearts, she shrank into a dusky corner with her knitting, happy if the evening passed without her brother saying, with a crude sarcasm, "Ask your Aunt Mehetabel about the beaux that used to come a-sparkin' her!" or, "Mehetabel, how was't when you was in love with Abel Cummings?" As a matter of fact, she had been the same at twenty as at sixty, a mouselike little creature, too shy for anyone to notice, or to raise her eyes for a moment and wish for a life of her own.

Her sister-in-law, a big hearty housewife, who ruled indoors with as autocratic a sway as did her husband on the farm, was rather kind in an absent, offhand way to the shrunken little old woman, and it was through her that Mehetabel was able to enjoy the one pleasure of her life. Even as a girl she had been clever with her needle in the way of patching bedquilts. More than

BROKEN STAR

Thoughts of the upcoming county fair encouraged ambitious quilters to do their best work. The winner of the annual quilt competition at the fair would earn a moment of fame and the respect of her fellow quilters. This richly colored and intricately stitched quilt from Lovina's Stitchery in Strasburg, Pennsylvania looks as though it would have been a contender. (Photograph © Keith Baum/ BaumsAway!)

that she could never learn to do. The garments which she made for herself were lamentable affairs, and she was humbly grateful for any help in the bewildering business of putting them together. But in patchwork she enjoyed a tepid importance. She could really do that as well as anyone else. During years of devotion to this one art she had accumulated a considerable store of quilting patterns. Sometimes the neighbors would send over and ask "Miss Mehetabel" for the loan of her sheaf-of-wheat design or the double-star pattern. It was with an agreeable flutter at being able to help someone that she went to the dresser, in her bare little room under the eaves, and drew out from her crowded portfolio the pattern desired.

She never knew how her great idea came to her. Sometimes she thought she must have dreamed it, some-times she even wondered reverently, in the phraseology of the weekly prayer-meeting, if it had not been "sent" to her. She never admitted to herself that she could have thought of it without other help. It was too great, too ambitious, too lofty a project for her humble mind to have conceived. Even when she finished drawing the design with her own fingers, she gazed at it incredulously, not daring to believe that it could indeed be her handiwork. At first it seemed to her only like a lovely but unreal dream. For a long time she did not once think of putting an actual quilt together following that pattern, even though she herself had invented it. It was not that she feared the prodigious effort that would be needed to get those tiny, oddly shaped pieces of bright-colored material sewed together with the perfection of fine workmanship needed. No, she thought zestfully and eagerly of such endless effort, her heart uplifted by her vision of the mosaic-beauty of the whole creation as she saw it, when she shut her eyes to dream of it—that complicated, splendidly difficult pattern—good enough for the angels in heaven to quilt.

But as she dreamed, her nimble old fingers reached out longingly to turn her dream into reality. She began to think adventurously of trying it out—it would perhaps not be too selfish to make one square—just one unit of her design to see how it would look. She dared do nothing in the household where she was a dependent, without asking permission. With a heart full of hope and fear thumping furiously against her old ribs, she approached the mistress of the house on churning-day, knowing with the innocent guile of a child that the country woman was apt to be in a good temper while working over the fragrant butter in the cool cellar.

Sophia listened absently to her sister-in-law's halting petition. "Why, yes, Mehetabel," she said, leaning far down into the huge churn for the last golden morsels "why, yes, start another quilt if you want to. I've got a lot of pieces from the spring sewing that will work in real good." Mehetabel tried honestly to make her see that this would be no common quilt, but her limited vocabulary and her emotion stood between her and expression. At last Sophia said, with a kindly impatience: "Oh, there! Don't bother me. I never could keep track of your quiltin' patterns, anyhow. I don't care what pattern you go by."

Mehetabel rushed back up the steep attic stairs to her room, and in a joyful agitation began preparations for the work of her life. Her very first stitches showed her that it was even better than she hoped. By some heaven-sent inspiration she had invented a pattern beyond which no patchwork quilt could go.

She had but little time during the daylight hours filled with the incessant household drudgery. After dark she did not dare to sit up late at night lest she burn too much candle. It was weeks before the little square began to show the pattern. Then Mehetabel was in a fever to finish it. She was too conscientious to shirk even the smallest part of her share of the housework, but she rushed through it now so fast that she was panting as she climbed the stairs to her little room.

Every time she opened the door, no matter what weather hung outside the one small window, she always saw the little room flooded with sunshine. She

smiled to herself as she bent over the innumerable scraps of cotton cloth on her work table. Already—to her—they were ranged in orderly, complex, mosaic-beauty.

Finally she could wait no longer, and one evening ventured to bring her work down beside the fire where the family sat, hoping that good fortune would give her a place near the tallow candles on the mantelpiece. She had reached the last corner of that first square and her needle flew in and out, in and out, with nervous speed. To her relief no one noticed her. By bedtime she had only a few more stitches to add.

As she stood up with the others, the square fell from her trembling old hands and fluttered to the table. Sophia glanced at it carelessly. "Is that the new quilt you said you wanted to start?" she asked, yawning. "Looks like a real pretty pattern. Let's see it."

Up to that moment Mehetabel had labored in the purest spirit of selfless adoration of an ideal. The emotional shock given her by Sophia's cry of admiration as she held the work towards the candle to examine it, was as much astonishment as joy to Mehetabel.

"Land's sakes!" cried her sister-in-law. "Why,

LABOR OF LOVE
Long hours spent patiently piecing and quilting can produce more than just a beautiful quilt. The finished work also gives a feeling of contentment and pride in a job well done. (Photograph © Daniel Dempster)

©Sandi Wickersham Resnick

"County Fair and Quilt Show"
Sandi Wickersham does an outstanding job of capturing the hustle and bustle of a typical small-town community event in this captivating painting. A childhood version of the artist herself and her black Labrador retriever, Coalie, appear in each of her works—here, a youthful, pigtailed Wickersham and her faithful canine companion sit atop a horse in the center of the action. (Artwork © Sandi Wickersham)

Mehetabel Elwell, where did you git that pattern?"

"I made it up," said Mehetabel. She spoke quietly but she was trembling.

"No!" exclaimed Sophia. "Did you! Why, I never see such a pattern in my life. Girls, come here and see what your Aunt Mehetabel is doing."

The three tall daughters turned back reluctantly from the stairs. "I never could seem to take much interest in patchwork quilts," said one. Already the old-time skill born of early pioneer privation and the craving for beauty, had gone out of style.

"No, nor I neither!" answered Sophia. "But a stone image would take an interest in this pattern. Honest, Mehetabel, did you really think of it yourself?" She held it up closer to her eyes and went on, "And how under the sun and stars did you ever git your courage up to start in a-making it? Land! Look at all those tiny squinchy little seams! Why, the wrong side ain't a thing *but* seams! Yet the good side's just like a picture, so smooth you'd think 'twas woven that way. Only nobody could."

The girls looked at it right side, wrong side, and echoed their mother's exclamations. Mr. Elwell himself came over to see what they were discussing. "Well, I declare!" he said, looking at his sister with eyes more approving than she could ever remember. "I don't know a thing about patchwork quilts, but to my eye that beats old Mis' Andrew's quilt that got the blue ribbon so many times at the County Fair."

As she lay that night in her narrow hard bed, too proud, too excited to sleep, Mehetabel's heart swelled and tears of joy ran down from her old eyes.

The next day her sister-in-law astonished her by taking the huge pan of potatoes out of her lap and setting one of the younger children to peeling them. "Don't you want to go on with that quiltin' pattern?" she said. "I'd kind o' like to see how you're goin' to make the grapevine design come out on the corner."

For the first time in her life the dependent old maid contradicted her powerful sister-in-law. Quickly and jealously she said, "It's not a grapevine. It's a sort of curlicue I made up."

"Well, it's nice-looking anyhow," said Sophia pacifyingly. "I never could have made it up."

By the end of the summer the family interest had risen so high that Mehetabel was given for herself a little round table in the sitting room, for *her*, where she could keep her pieces and use odd minutes for her work. She almost wept over such kindness and resolved firmly not to take advantage of it. She went on faithfully with her monotonous housework, not neglecting a corner. But the atmosphere of her world was changed. Now things had a meaning. Through the longest task of washing milk-pans, there rose a rainbow of promise. She took her place by the little table and put the thimble on her knotted, hard finger with the solemnity of a priestess performing a rite.

She was even able to bear with some degree of dignity the honor of having the minister and the minister's wife comment admiringly on her great project. The family felt quite proud of Aunt Mehetabel as Minister Bowman had said it was work as fine as any he had ever seen, "and he didn't know but finer!" The remark was repeated verbatim to the neighbors in the following weeks when they dropped in and examined in a perverse Vermontish silence some astonishingly difficult tour de force which Mehetabel had just finished.

The Elwells especially plumed themselves on the slow progress of the quilt. "Mehetabel has been to work on that corner for six weeks, come Tuesday, and she ain't half done yet," they explained to visitors. They fell out of the way of always expecting her to be the one to run on errands, even for the children. "Don't bother your Aunt Mehetabel," Sophia would call. "Can't you see she's got to a ticklish place on the quilt?" The old woman sat straighter in her chair, held up her head. She was a part of the world at last. She joined in the conversation and her remarks were listened to. The children were even told to mind her when she asked them to do some service for her, although this she ventured to do but seldom.

One day some people from the next town, total strangers, drove up to the Elwell house and asked if they could inspect the wonderful quilt which they had heard about even down in their end of the valley. After that, Mehetabel's quilt came little by little to be one of the local sights. No visitor to town, whether he knew the Elwells or not, went away without having been to look at it. To make her presentable to strangers, the Elwells saw to it that their aunt was better dressed than she had ever been before. One of the girls made her a pretty little cap to wear on her thin white hair.

SIGNED AND DELIVERED

Signature quilts, which are made up of quilt blocks autographed by the hands that made them, were most popular in the mid 1800s. Also known as Friendship or Album quilts, they were typically made by a group of quilters and then presented as gifts on special occasions. The quilt pictured here was appliquéd and quilted in 1859. Many of its blocks feature a quilter's name that has been either handwritten in permanent ink or embroidered. (Courtesy of Washington County MN Historical Society, photograph by Tomy O'Brien)

A year went by and a quarter of the quilt was finished. A second year passed and half was done. The third year Mehetabel had pneumonia and lay ill for weeks and weeks, horrified by the idea that she might die before her work was completed. A fourth year and one could really see the grandeur of the whole design. In September of the fifth year, the entire family gathered around her to watch eagerly, as Mehetabel quilted the last stitches. The girls held it up by the four corners and they all looked at it in hushed silence.

Then Mr. Elwell cried as one speaking with authority, "By ginger! That's goin' to the County Fair!"

Mehetabel blushed a deep red. She had thought of this herself, but never would have spoken aloud of it.

"Yes indeed!" cried the family. One of the boys was dispatched to the house of a neighbor who was Chairman of the Fair Committee for their village. He came back beaming, "Of course he'll take it. Like's not it may git a prize, he says. But he's got to have it right off because all the things from our town are going tomorrow morning."

Even in her pride Mehetabel felt a pang as the bulky package was carried out of the house. As the days went on she felt lost. For years it had been her one thought. The little round stand had been heaped with a litter of bright-colored scraps. Now it was desolately bare. One of the neighbors who took the long journey to the Fair reported when he came back that the quilt was hung in a good place in a glass case in "Agricultural Hall." But that meant little to Mehetabel's ignorance of everything outside her brother's home. She drooped. The family noticed it. One day Sophia said kindly, "You feel sort o' lost without the quilt, don't you, Mehetabel?"

"They took it away so quick!" she said wistfully. "I hadn't hardly had one good look at it myself."

The Fair was to last a fortnight. At the beginning of the second week Mr. Elwell asked his sister how early she could get up in the morning.

"I dunno. Why?" she asked.

"Well, Thomas Ralston has got to drive to West Oldton to see a lawyer. That's four miles beyond the Fair. He says if you can git up so's to leave here at four in the morning he'll drive you to the Fair, leave you

EAGLE APPLIQUÉ QUILT
The appliqué method, which is executed by cutting out a fabric shape and sewing it onto a large piece of plain background fabric, allows the quilter a greater freedom of form than piecework. Traditional subject matter for the appliqué quilter included hearts, flowers, leaves, and birds, as is illustrated in this quilt, circa 1860, from the collection of Kitty Clark Cole. (Photograph © Keith Baum/BaumsAway!)

there for the day, and bring you back again at night." Mehetabel's face turned very white. Her eyes filled with tears. It was as though someone had offered her a ride in a golden chariot up to the gates of heaven. "Why, you can't *mean* it" she cried wildly. Her brother laughed. He could not meet her eyes. Even to his easy-going unimaginative indifference to his sister this was a revelation of the narrowness of her life in his home. "Oh, 'tain't so much—just to go to the Fair," he told her in some confusion, and then "Yes, sure I mean it. Go git your things ready, for it's tomorrow morning he wants to start."

A trembling, excited old woman stared all that night at the rafters. She who had never been more than six miles from home—it was to her like going into another world. She who had never seen anything more exciting than a church supper was to see the County Fair. She had never dreamed of doing it. She could not at all imagine what it would be like.

The next morning all the family rose early to see

her off. Perhaps her brother had not been the only one to be shocked by her happiness. As she tried to eat her breakfast they called out conflicting advice to her about what to see. Her brother said not to miss inspecting the stock, her nieces said the fancywork was the only thing worth looking at, Sophia told her to be sure to look at the display of preserves. Her nephews asked her to bring home an account of the trotting races.

The buggy drove up to the door, and she was helped in. The family ran to and fro with blankets, woolen tippet, a hot soapstone from the kitchen range. Her wraps were tucked about her. They all stood together and waved goodby as she drove out of the yard. She waved back, but she scarcely saw them. On her return home that evening she was ashy pale, and so stiff that her brother had to lift her out bodily. But her lips were set in a blissful smile. They crowded around her with questions until Sophia pushed them all aside. She told them Aunt Mehetabel was too tired to speak until she had had her supper. The young people held their tongues while she drank her tea, and absent-mindedly ate a scrap of toast with an egg. Then the old woman was helped into an easy chair before the fire. They gathered about her, eager for news of the great world, and Sophia said, "Now, come, Mehetabel, tell us all about it!"

Mehetabel drew a long breath. "It was just perfect!" she said. "Finer even than I thought. They've got it hanging up in the very middle of a sort o' closet made of glass, and one of the lower corners is ripped and turned back so's to show the seams on the wrong side."

"What?" asked Sophia, a little blankly.

"Why, the quilt!" said Mehetabel in surprise. "There are a whole lot of other ones in that room, but not one that can hold a candle to it, if I do say it who shouldn't. I heard lots of people say the same thing. You ought to have heard what the women said about that corner, Sophia. They said—well, I'd be ashamed to tell you what they said. I declare if I wouldn't!"

Mr. Elwell asked, "What did you think of that big ox we've heard so much about?"

"I didn't look at the stock," returned his sister indifferently. She turned to one of her nieces. "That set of pieces you gave me, Maria, from your red waist,

come out just lovely! I heard one woman say you could 'most smell the red roses."

"How did Jed Burgess' bay horse place in the mile trot?" asked Thomas.

"I didn't see the races."

"How about the preserves?" asked Sophia.

"I didn't see the preserves," said Mehetabel calmly.

Seeing that they were gazing at her with astonished faces she went on, to give them a reasonable explanation, "You see I went right to the room where the quilt was, and then I didn't want to leave it. It had been so long since I'd seen it. I had to look at it first real good myself, and then I looked at the others to see if there was any that could come up to it. Then the people begun comin' in and I got so interested in hearin' what they had to say I couldn't think of goin' anywheres else. I ate my lunch right there too, and I'm glad as can be I did, too; for what do you think?"—she gazed about her with kindling eyes. "While I stood there with a sandwich in one hand, didn't the head of the hull concern come in and open the glass door and pin a big bow of blue ribbon right in the middle of the quilt with a label on it, 'First Prize.'"

There was a stir of proud congratulation. Then Sophia returned to questioning, "Didn't you go to see anything else?"

"Why, no," said Mehetabel. "Only the quilt. Why should I?"

She fell into a reverie. As if it hung again before her eyes she saw the glory that shone around the creation of her hand and brain. She longed to make her listeners share the golden vision with her. She struggled for words. She fumbled blindly for unknown superlatives. "I tell you it looked like—" she began, and paused.

Vague recollections of hymnbook phrases came into her mind. They were the only kind of poetic expression she knew. But they were dismissed as being sacrilegious to use for something in real life. Also as not being nearly striking enough.

Finally, "I tell you it looked real *good*," she assured them and sat staring into the fire, on her tired old face the supreme content of an artist who has realized his ideal.

The Value of a Quilt from the Memories of a Former Kid

According to most children, a prize-winning quilt should not be judged on how tiny its stitches are, or how symmetrical its design is, but how toasty it will keep your toes on a frigid winter night.

Artist Bob Artley has shared his childhood recollections of life on the farm with readers through a syndicated cartoon series called "Memories of a Former Kid" for several decades. Now collected into books such as *Cartoons I*, *Cartoons II*, and *A Book of Chores as Remembered by a Former Kid*, the drawings bring near-forgotten days on the farm back to the reader.

In these cartoons, Bob Artley recalls the warmth and weight of the quilts of his youth.

Quilting on the Rebound

By Terry McMillan

MOST PEOPLE WOULD prescribe a box of chocolates or a half-gallon of ice cream to cure a broken heart, but in the short story "Quilting on the Rebound," Terry McMillan writes that quilting is the best medicine.

McMillan, a resident of San Francisco, California, has had her share of good times and bad. The author has enjoyed great acclaim for novels like *Waiting to Exhale*, *How Stella Got Her Groove Back*, and her latest book, *A Day Late and a Dollar Short*. In the midst of her success, however, McMillan had to deal with the loss of both her mother and her best friend in the mid-1990s. Writing has helped her get through some difficult years.

There are many cures that will soothe the soul. For Terry McMillan, it is the pen; for Marilyn, the heroine of "Quilting on the Rebound," it is a needle, thread, and a sharp pair of fabric shears.

■ ■ ■

HIDDEN HISTORY
Few nineteenth century African American quilts are documented as such, since their patterns were often traditional and difficult to distinguish from European American quilts. This Log Cabin Light and Dark variation was completed by Rosie L. Wilkins of Muskegon, Michigan, in 1989. (Courtesy of Michigan State University Museum)

Five years ago, I did something I swore I'd never do—went out with someone I worked with. We worked for a large insurance company in L.A. Richard was a senior examiner and I was a chief under-writer. The first year, we kept it a secret, and not because we were afraid of jeopardizing our jobs. Richard was twenty-six and I was thirty-four. By the second year, everybody knew it anyway and nobody seemed to care. We'd been going out for three years when I realized that this relationship was going nowhere. I probably could've dated him for the rest of my life and he'd have been satisfied. Richard had had a long reputation for being a Don Juan of sorts, until he met me. I cooled his heels. His name was also rather ironic, because he looked like a black Richard Gere. The fact that I was older than he was made him feel powerful in a sense, and he believed that he could do for me what men my own age apparently couldn't. But that wasn't true. He was a challenge. I wanted to see if I could make his head and heart turn 360 degrees, and I did. I blew his young mind in bed, but he also charmed me into loving him until I didn't care how old he was.

Richard thought I was exotic because I have slanted eyes, high cheekbones, and full lips. Even though my mother is Japanese and my dad is black, I inherited most of his traits. My complexion is dark, my hair is nappy, and I'm five six. I explained to Richard that I was proud of both of my heritages, but he has insisted on thinking of me as being mostly Japanese. Why, I don't know. I grew up in a black neighborhood in L.A., went to Dorsey High School—which was predominantly black, Asian, and Hispanic—and most of my friends are black. I've never even considered going out with anyone other than black men.

My mother, I'm glad to say, is not the stereotypical passive Japanese wife either. She's been the head nurse in Kaiser's cardiovascular unit for over twenty years, and my dad has his own landscaping business, even though he should've retired years ago. My mother liked Richard and his age didn't bother her, but she believed that if a man loved you he should marry you. Simple as that. On the other hand, my dad didn't care who I married just as long as it was soon. I'll be the first to admit that I was a spoiled-rotten brat because my mother had had three miscarriages before she finally had me and I was used to getting everything I wanted. Richard was no exception. "Give him the ultimatum," my mother had said, if he didn't propose by my thirty-eighth birthday.

But I didn't have to. I got pregnant.

We were having dinner at an Italian restaurant when I told him. "You want to get married, don't you?" he'd said.

"Do you?" I asked.

He was picking through his salad and then he jabbed his fork into a tomato. "Why not, we were headed in that direction anyway, weren't we?" He did not eat his tomato but laid his fork down on the side of the plate. I swallowed a spoonful of my clam chowder, then asked, "Were we?"

"You know the answer to that. But hell, now's as good a time as any. We're both making good money, and sometimes all a man needs is a little incentive." He didn't look at me when he said this, and his voice was strained. "Look" he said, "I've had a pretty shitty day, haggling with one of the adjusters, so forgive me if I don't appear to be boiling over with excitement. I am happy about this. Believe me, I am," he said, and picked up a single piece of lettuce with a different fork and put it into his mouth.

My parents were thrilled when I told them, but my mother was nevertheless suspicious. "Funny how this baby pop up, isn't it?" she'd said.

"What do you mean?"

"You know exactly what I mean. I hope baby doesn't backfire."

I ignored what she'd just said. "Will you help me make my dress?" I asked.

"Yes," she said. "But we must hurry."

My parents—who are far from well off—went all out for this wedding. My mother didn't want anyone to know I was pregnant, and to be honest, I didn't either. The age difference was enough to handle as it was. Close to three hundred people had been invited, and my parents had spent an astronomical amount of money to rent a country club in Marina Del Rey. "At your age," my dad had said, "I hope you'll only be doing this once." Richard's parents insisted on taking care of the caterer and the liquor, and my parents didn't object. I paid for the cake.

About a month before the Big Day, I was meeting Richard at the jeweler because he'd picked out my ring and wanted to make sure I liked it. He was so excited, he sounded like a little boy. It was beautiful, but I told him he didn't have to spend four thousand dollars on my wedding ring. "You're worth it," he'd said and kissed me on the cheek. When we got to the parking lot, he opened my door, and stood there staring at me. "Four more weeks," he said, "and you'll be my wife." He didn't smile when he said it, but closed the door and walked around to the driver's side and got in. He'd driven four whole blocks without saying a word and his knuckles were almost white because of how tight he was holding the steering wheel.

"Is something wrong, Richard?" I asked him.

"What would make you think that?" he said. Then he laid on the horn because someone in front of us hadn't moved and the light had just barely turned green.

"Richard, we don't have to go through with this, you know."

"I know we don't *have* to, but it's the right thing to do, and I'm going to do it. So don't worry, we'll be happy."

But I *was* worried.

I'd been doing some shopping at the Beverly Center when I started getting these stomach cramps while I was going up the escalator, so I decided to sit down. I walked over to one of the little outside cafés and I felt something lock inside my stomach, so I pulled out a chair. Moments later my skirt felt like it was wet. I got up and looked at the chair and saw a small red puddle. I sat back down and started crying. I didn't know what to do. Then a punkish-looking girl came over and asked if I was okay. "I'm pregnant, and I've just bled all over this chair," I said.

"Can I do something for you? Do you want me to call an ambulance?" She was popping chewing gum and I wanted to snatch it out of her mouth.

By this time at least four other women had gathered around me. The punkish-looking girl told them about my condition. One of the women said, "Look, let's get her to the rest room. She's probably having a miscarriage."

Two of the women helped me up and all four of them formed a circle around me, then slowly led me to the ladies' room. I told them that I wasn't in any pain, but they were still worried. I closed the stall door, pulled down two toilet seat covers and sat down. I felt as if I had to go, so I pushed. Something plopped out of me and it made a splash. I was afraid to get up but I got up and looked at this large dark mass that looked like liver. I put my hand over my mouth because I knew that was my baby.

"Are you okay in there?"

I went to open my mouth, but the joint in my jawbone clicked and my mouth wouldn't move.

"Are you okay in there, miss?"

I wanted to answer, but I couldn't.

"Miss," I heard her banging on the door.

I felt my mouth loosen. "It's gone," I said. "It's gone."

"Honey, open the door," someone said, but I couldn't move. Then I heard myself say, "I think I need a sanitary pad." I was staring into the toilet bowl when I felt a hand hit my leg. "Here, are you sure you're okay in there?"

"Yes," I said. Then I flushed the toilet with my foot and watched my future disappear. I put the pad on and reached inside my shopping bag, pulled out a Raiders sweatshirt I'd bought for Richard and tied it around my waist. When I came out, all of the women were waiting for me. "Would you like us to call your husband? Where are you parked? Do you feel light-headed, dizzy?"

"No, I'm fine, really, and thank you so much for your concern. I appreciate it, but I feel okay."

I drove home in a daze and when I opened the door to my condo, I was glad I lived alone. I sat on the couch from one o'clock to four o'clock without moving. When I finally got up, it felt as if I'd only been there for five minutes

SHADES OF BLUE
The color scheme of this Lily quilt has a calming effect. The heart motif in the quilting stitches indicates that the quilt may have been made for a woman approaching her wedding day. (Photograph © Jerry Irwin)

I didn't tell Richard. I didn't tell anybody. I bled for three days before I went to see my doctor. He scolded me because I'd gotten some kind of an infection and had to be prescribed antibiotics, then he sent me to the outpatient clinic, where I had to have a D & C.

Two weeks later, I had a surprise shower and got enough gifts to fill the housewares department at Bullock's. One of my old girlfriends, Gloria, came all the way from Phoenix, and I hadn't seen her in three years. I hardly recognized her, she was as big as a house. "You don't know how lucky you are, girl," she'd said to me. "I wish I could be here for the wedding but Tarik is having his sixteenth birthday party and I am not leaving a bunch of teenagers alone in my house. Besides, I'd probably have a heart attack watching you or anybody else walk down an aisle in white. Come to think of it, I can't even remember the last time I went to a wedding."

"Me either," I said.

"I know you're gonna try to get pregnant in a hurry, right?" she asked, holding out her wrist with the watch on it.

Two to tango
This antique Pineapple variation quilt illustrates that piecing a quilt with just two colors of fabric can have a dramatic effect. (Courtesy of Washington County MN Historical Society, photograph by Tomy O'Brien)

I tried to smile. "I'm going to work on it," I said.

"Well, who knows?" Gloria said, laughing. "Maybe one day you'll be coming to my wedding. We may both be in wheelchairs, but you never know."

"I'll be there," I said.

All Richard said when he saw the gifts was, "What are we going to do with all this stuff? Where are we going to put it?"

"It depends on where we're going to live," I said, which we hadn't even talked about. My condo was big enough and so was his apartment.

"It doesn't matter to me, but I think we should wait a while before buying a house. A house is a big investment, you know. Thirty years." He gave me a quick look.

"Are you getting cold feet?" I blurted out.

"No, I'm not getting cold feet. It's just that in two weeks we're going to be man and wife, and it takes a little getting used to the idea, that's all."

"Are you having doubts about the idea of it?"

"No."

"Are you sure?"

"I'm sure," he said.

I didn't stop bleeding, so I took some vacation time to relax, and finish my dress. I worked on it day and night and was doing all the beadwork by hand. My mother was spending all her free time at my place trying to make sure everything was happening on schedule. A week before the Big Day I was trying on my gown for the hundredth time when the phone rang. I thought it might be Richard, since he hadn't called me in almost forty-eight hours, and when I finally called him and left a message, he still hadn't returned my call. My father said this was normal.

"Hello," I said.

"I think you should talk to Richard." It was his mother.

"About what?" I asked.

"He's not feeling very well," was all she said.

"What's wrong with him?"

"I don't know for sure. I think it's his stomach."

"Is he sick?"

"I don't know. Call him."

"I did call him but he hasn't returned my call."

"Keep trying," she said.

So I called him at work, but his secretary said he wasn't there. I called him at home and he wasn't there either, so I left another message and for the next three hours I was a wreck, waiting to hear from him. I knew something was wrong.

I gave myself a facial, a manicure and pedicure and watched Oprah Winfrey while I waited by the phone. It didn't ring. My mother was downstairs hemming one of the bridesmaid's dresses. I went down to get myself a glass of wine. "How you feeling, Marilyn Monroe?" she asked.

"What do you mean, how am I feeling? I'm feeling fine."

"All I meant was you awful lucky with no morning sickness or anything, but I must say, hormones changing because you getting awfully irritating."

"I'm sorry, Ma."

"It's okay. I had jitters too."

I went back upstairs and closed my bedroom door, then went into my bathroom. I put the wineglass on the side of the bathtub and decided to take a bubble bath in spite of the bleeding. I must have poured half a bottle of Secreti in. The water was too hot but I got in anyway. Call, dammit, call. just then the phone rang and scared me half to death. I was hyperventilating and couldn't say much except, "Hold on a minute," while I caught my breath.

"Marilyn?" Richard was saying. "Marilyn?" But before I had a chance to answer he blurted out what must have been on his mind all along. "Please don't be mad at me, but I can't do this. I'm not ready. I wanted to do the right thing, but I'm only twenty-nine years old. I've got my whole life ahead of me. I'm not ready to be a father yet. I'm not ready to be anybody's husband either, and I'm scared. Everything is happening too fast. I know you think I'm being a coward, and you're probably right. But I've been having nightmares, Marilyn. Do you hear me, nightmares about being imprisoned. I haven't been able to sleep through the night. I doze off and wake up dripping wet. And my stomach. It's in knots. Believe me, Marilyn, its not that I don't love you because I do. It's not that I don't care about the baby, because I do. I just can't do this right now. I can't make this kind of commitment right now. I'm sorry. Marilyn? Marilyn, are you still there?"

I dropped the portable phone in the bathtub and got out.

My mother heard me screaming and came tearing into the room. "What happened?" I was dripping wet and ripping the pearls off my dress but somehow I managed to tell her.

"He come to his senses," she said. "This happen a lot. He just got cold feet, but give him day or two. He not mean it."

Three days went by and he didn't call. My mother stayed with me and did everything she could to console me, but by that time I'd already flushed the ring down the toilet.

"I hope you don't lose baby behind this," she said.

"I've already lost the baby," I said.

"What?"

"A month ago."

Her mouth was wide open. She found the sofa with her hand and sat down. "Marilyn," she said and let out an exasperated sigh.

"I couldn't tell anybody."

"Why not tell somebody? Why not me, your mother?"

"Because I was too scared."

"Scared of what?"

"That Richard might change his mind."

"Man love you, dead baby not change his mind."

"I was going to tell him after we got married."

"I not raise you to be dishonest."

"I know."

"No man in world worth lying about something like this. How could you?"

"I don't know."

"I told you it backfire, didn't I?"

For weeks I couldn't eat or sleep. At first, all I did was think about what was wrong with me. I was too old. For him. No. He didn't care about my age. It was the gap in my teeth, or my slight overbite, from all those years I used to suck my thumb. But he never mentioned anything about it and I was really the only one who seemed to notice. I was flat-chested. I had cellulite. My ass was square instead of round. I wasn't exciting as I used to be in bed. No. I was still good in bed, that much I did know. I couldn't cook. I was a terrible housekeeper. That was it. If you couldn't cook and keep a clean house, what kind of wife would you make?

I had to make myself stop thinking about my infinite flaws, so I started quilting again. I was astonished at how radiant the colors were that I was choosing, how unconventional and wild the patterns were. With-

out even realizing it, I was fusing Japanese and African motifs and was quite excited by the results. My mother was worried about me, even though I had actually stopped bleeding for two whole weeks. Under the circumstances, she thought that my obsession with quilting was not normal, so she forced me to go to the doctor. He gave me some kind of an antidepressant, which I refused to take. I told him I was not depressed, I was simply hurt. Besides, a pill wasn't any antidote or consolation for heartache.

I began to patronize just about every fabric store in downtown Los Angeles, and while I listened to the humming of my machine, and concentrated on designs that I couldn't believe I was creating, it occurred to me that I wasn't suffering from heartache at all. I actually felt this incredible sense of relief. As if I didn't have to anticipate anything else happening that was outside of my control. And when I did grieve, it was always because I had lost a child, not a future husband.

I also heard my mother all day long on my phone, lying about some tragedy that had happened and apologizing for any inconvenience it may have caused. And I watched her, bent over at the dining room table, writing hundreds of thank-you notes to the people she was returning gifts to. She even signed my name. My father wanted to kill Richard. "He was too young, and he wasn't good enough for you anyway," he said. "This is really a blessing in disguise."

I took a leave of absence from my job because there was no way in hell I could face those people, and the thought of looking at Richard infuriated me. I was not angry at him for not marrying me, I was angry at him for not being honest, for the way he handled it all. He even had the nerve to come over without calling. I had opened the door but wouldn't let him inside. He was nothing but a little pip-squeak. A handsome, five-foot-seven-inch pip-squeak.

"Marilyn, look, we need to talk."

"About what?"

"Us. The baby."

"There is no baby."

"What do you mean, there's no baby?"

"It died."

"You mean you got rid of it?"

"No, I lost it."

"I'm sorry, Marilyn," he said and put his head

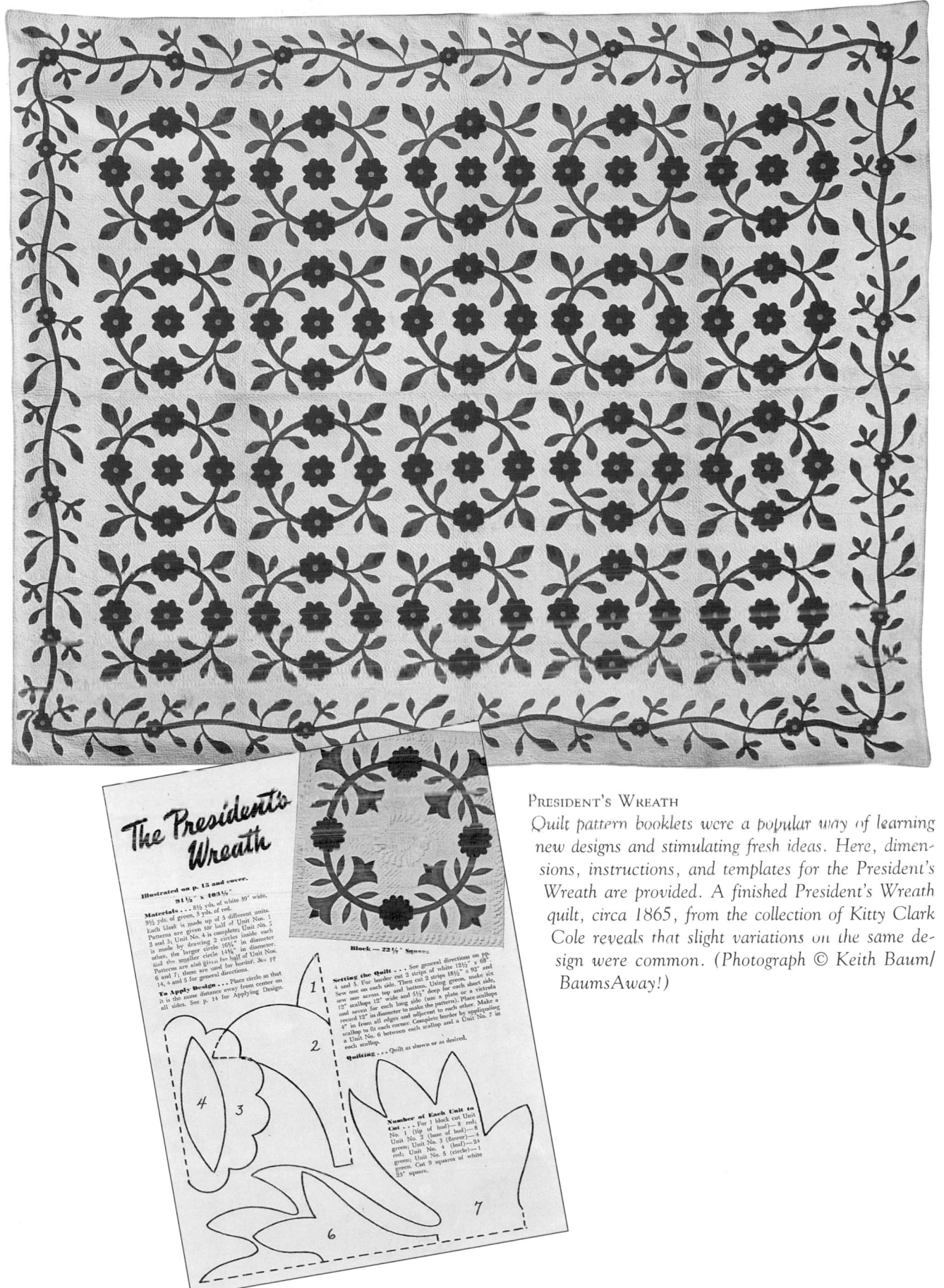

PRESIDENT'S WREATH

Quilt pattern booklets were a popular way of learning new designs and stimulating fresh ideas. Here, dimensions, instructions, and templates for the President's Wreath are provided. A finished President's Wreath quilt, circa 1865, from the collection of Kitty Clark Cole reveals that slight variations on the same design were common. (Photograph © Keith Baum/BaumsAway!)

"Farm Fresh Antiques"
In this rendition of a crisp autumn afternoon, folk artist Sandi Wickersham
brings to life an antique store with a
stack of quilts ready for sale. Quilts are
often lauded for their roles as practical bedcovers and outlets for self-
expression, but they have also been
historically important for their economic role in the lives of women.
Quilters who sold their wares not only
possessed a valuable domestic skill but
a measure of financial freedom as well.
(Artwork © Sandi Wickersham)

FARM FRESH
ANTIQUES

FRESH
PRODUCE

MUMS

Auction
every
Monday

VALLEY DAIRY

DELIVERIES

© Sandi Wickersham

down. How touching, I thought. "This is all my fault."

"It's not your fault, Richard."

"Look. Can I come in?"

"For what?"

"I want to talk. I need to talk to you."

"About what?"

"About us."

"Us?"

"Yes, us. I don't want it to be over between us. I just need more time, that's all."

"Time for what?"

"To make sure this is what I want to do."

"Take all the time you need," I said and slammed the door in his face. He rang the buzzer again, but I just told him to get lost and leave me alone.

I went upstairs and sat at my sewing machine. I turned the light on, then picked up a piece of purple and terra-cotta cloth. I slid it under the pressure foot and dropped it. I pressed down on the pedal and watched the needle zigzag. The stitches were too loose so I tightened the tension. Richard is going to be the last in a series of mistakes I've made when it comes to picking a man. I've picked the wrong one too many times, like a bad habit that's too hard to break. I haven't had the best of luck when it comes to keeping them either, and to be honest, Richard was the one who lasted the longest.

When I got to the end of the fabric, I pulled the top and bobbin threads together and cut them on the thread cutter. Then I bent down and picked up two different pieces. They were black and purple. I always want what I can't have or what I'm not supposed to have. So what did I do? Created a pattern of choosing men that I knew would be a challenge. Richard's was his age. But the others—all of them from Alex to William—were all afraid of something: namely committing to one woman. All I wanted to do was seduce them hard enough—emotionally, mentally, and physically—so they wouldn't even be aware that they were committing to anything. I just wanted them to crave me, and no one else but me. I wanted to be their healthiest addiction. But it was a lot harder to do than I thought. What I found out was that men are a hard nut to crack.

But some of them weren't. When I was in my late twenties, early thirties—before I got serious and realized I wanted a long-term relationship—I'd had at least twenty different men fall in love with me, but of course these were the ones I didn't want. They were the ones who after a few dates or one rousing night in bed, ordained themselves my "man" or were too quick to want to marry me, and even some considered me their "property." When it was clear that I was dealing with a different species of man, a hungry element, before I got in too deep, I'd tell them almost immediately that I hope they wouldn't mind my being bisexual or my being unfaithful because I was in no hurry to settle down with one man, or that I had a tendency of always falling for my man's friends. Could they tolerate that? I even went so far as to tell them that I hoped having herpes wouldn't cause a problem, that I wasn't really all that trustworthy because I was a habitual liar, and that if they wanted the whole truth they should find themselves another woman. I told them that I didn't even think I was good enough for them, and they should do themselves a favor, find a woman who's truly worthy of having such a terrific man.

I had it down to a science, but by the time I met Richard, I was tired of lying and conniving. I was sick of the games. I was whipped, really, and allowed myself to relax and be vulnerable because I knew I was getting old.

When Gloria called to see how my honeymoon went, I told her the truth about everything. She couldn't believe it. "Well, I thought I'd heard 'em all, but this one takes the cake. How you holding up?"

"I'm hanging in there."

"This is what makes you want to castrate a man."

"Not really, Gloria."

"I know. But you know what I mean. Some of them have a lot of nerve, I swear they do. But really, Marilyn, how are you feeling for real, baby?"

"I'm getting my period every other week, but I'm quilting again, which is a good sign."

"First of all, take your behind back to that doctor and find out why you're still bleeding like this. And, honey, making quilts is no consolation for a broken heart. It sounds like you could use some R & R. Why don't you come visit me for a few days?"

I looked around my room, which had piles and piles of cloth and half-sewn quilts, from where I'd changed my mind. Hundreds of different colored thread were all over the carpet, and the satin stitch I was

"Every Quilting Need"
This vintage advertisement from Coats & Clark promises that their thread would suit any quilting task. But every seasoned quilter knows that it would be impossible to meet every quilting need—just one more yard of fabric is always a necessity.

trying out wasn't giving me the effect I thought it would. I could use a break, I thought. I could. "You know what?" I said. "I think I will."

"Good, and bring me one of those tacky quilts. I don't have anything to snuggle up with in the winter, and contrary to popular belief, it does get cold here come December."

I liked Phoenix and Tempe, but I fell in love with Scottsdale. Not only was it beautiful but I couldn't believe how inexpensive it was to live in the entire area, which was all referred to as the Valley. I have to thank Gloria for being such a lifesaver. She took me

to her beauty salon and gave me a whole new look. She chopped off my hair, and one of the guys in her shop showed me how to put on my makeup in a way that would further enhance what assets he insisted I had.

We drove to Tucson, to Canyon Ranch for what started out as a simple Spa Renewal Day. But we ended up spending three glorious days and had the works. I had an herbal wrap, where they wrapped my entire body in hot thin linen that had been steamed. Then they rolled me up in flannel blankets and put a cold wash cloth on my forehead. I sweated in the dark for a half hour. Gloria didn't do this because she said she was claustrophobic and didn't want to be wrapped up in anything where she couldn't move. I had a deep-muscle and shiatsu massage on two different days. We steamed. We Jacuzzied. We both had a mud facial, and then this thing called aroma therapy—where they put distilled essences from flowers and herbs on your face and you look like a different person when they finish. On the last day, we got this Persian Body Polish where they actually buffed our skin with crushed pearl creams, sprayed us with some kind of herbal spray, then used an electric brush to make us tingle. We had our hands and feet moisturized and put in heated gloves and booties and by the time we left, we couldn't believe we were the same women.

In Phoenix, Gloria took me to yet another resort where we listened to live music. We went to see a stupid movie and I actually laughed. Then we went on a two-day shopping spree and I charged whatever I felt like. I even bought her son a pair of eighty-dollar sneakers, and I'd only seen him twice in my life.

I felt like I'd gotten my spirit back, so when I got home, I told my parents I'd had it with the smog, the traffic, the gangs, and L.A. in general. My mother said, "You cannot run from heartache," but I told her I wasn't running from anything. I put my condo on the market, and in less than a month, it sold for four times what I paid for it. I moved in with my mother and father, asked for a job transfer for health reasons, and when it came through, three months later, I moved to Scottsdale.

The town house I bought feels like a house. It's twice the size of the one I had and cost less than half of what I originally spent. My complex is pretty standard for Scottsdale. It has two pools and four tennis courts. It also has vaulted ceilings, wall-to-wall carpet, two fireplaces, and a garden bathtub with a Jacuzzi in it. The kitchen has an island in the center and I've got a 180-degree view of Phoenix and mountains. It also has three bedrooms. One I sleep in, one I use for sewing, and the other is for guests.

I made close to forty thousand dollars after I sold my condo, so I sent four to my parents because the money they'd put down for the wedding was nonrefundable. They really couldn't afford that kind of loss. The rest I put in an IRA and CDs until I could figure out something better to do with it.

I hated my new job. I had to accept a lower-level position and less money, which didn't bother me all that much at first. The office, however, was much smaller and full of rednecks who couldn't stand the thought of a black woman working over them. I was combing the classifieds, looking for a comparable job, but the job market in Phoenix is nothing close to what it is in L.A.

But thank God Gloria's got a big mouth. She'd been boasting to all of her clients about my quilts, had even hung the one I'd given her on the wall at the shop, and the next thing I know I'm getting so many orders I couldn't keep up with them. That's when she asked me why didn't I consider opening my own shop. That never would've occurred to me, but what did I have to lose?

She introduced me to Bernadine, a friend of hers who was an accountant. Bernadine in turn introduced me to a good lawyer and he helped me draw up all the papers. Over the next four months, she helped me devise what turned out to be a strong marketing and advertising plan. I rented an 800-square-foot space in the same shopping center where Gloria's shop is, and opened Quiltworks, Etc.

It wasn't long before I realized I needed to get some help, so I hired two seamstresses. They took a lot of the strain off of me, and I was able to take some jewelry-making classes and even started selling small pieces in the shop. Gloria gave me this tacky T-shirt for my thirty-ninth birthday, which gave me the idea to experiment with making them. Because I go overboard in everything I do, I went out and spent a fortune on every color of metallic and acrylic fabric paint they made. I bought one hundred 100 percent cotton heavy-duty men's T-shirts and discovered other uses for sponges, plastic, spray bottles, rolling pins, lace, and even old envelopes. I was having a great time because I'd never felt this kind of excitement and gratification doing anything until now.

I'd been living here a year when I found out that Richard had married another woman who worked in our office. I wanted to hate him, but I didn't. I wanted to be angry, but I wasn't. I didn't feel anything toward him, but I sent him a quilt and a wedding card to congratulate him, just because.

To be honest, I've been so busy with my shop, I haven't even thought about men. I don't even miss having sex unless I really just *think* about it. My libido must be evaporating, because when I *do* think about it, I just make quilts or jewelry or paint T-shirts and the feeling goes away. Some of my best ideas come at these moments.

Basically, I'm doing everything I can to make Marilyn feel good. And at thirty-nine years old my body needs tightening, so I joined a health club and started working out three to four times a week. Once in a while, I babysit for Bernadine, and it breaks my heart when I think about the fact that I don't have a child of my own. Sometimes, Gloria and I go out to hear some music. I frequent most of the major art galleries, go to just about every football and basketball game at Arizona State, and see at least one movie a week.

I am rarely bored. Which is why I've decided that at this point in my life, I really don't care if I ever get married. I've learned that I don't need a man in order to survive, that a man is nothing but an intrusion, and they require too much energy. I don't think they're worth it. Besides, they have too much power, and from what I've seen, they always seem to abuse it. The one thing I do have is power over my own life. I like it this way, and I'm not about to give it up for something that may not last.

The one thing I do want is to have a baby. Someone I could love who would love me back with no strings attached. But at thirty-nine, I know my days are numbered. I'd be willing to do it alone, if that's the only way I can have one. But right now, my life is almost full. It's fun, it's secure, and it's safe. About the only thing I'm concerned about these days is whether or not it's time to branch out into leather.

HAWAIIAN SCRAP QUILT

Every Hawaiian island has its own flower and color associated with it, and many Hawaiian quilters follow these symbolic colors and designs when making a quilt. Patterns created by Hawaiian quiltmakers are very personal, and one must have the permission of the originator before copying her quilt design. This scrap quilt was made in 1997 by members of Ka Hui Kapu Apana O Wasimea of Waimea, Hawaii. (Courtesy of Michigan State University Museum)

©Sandi Wickersham Resnik

CHAPTER 4

A Community of Quilters

" . . . Quilting Day belonged to the women. It was all right for a man to deliver his wife at a quilting, but he had to get away as fast as he could. If he went to the house and sat down with the womenfolks and tried to be sociable, they'd have run him out with brooms."
—Homer Croy, Country Cured, 1943

Quilts have been binding women together for centuries. Whether it be through the simple exchange of patterns or a shared bag of fabric scraps, quilting is a true community effort.

Often, it is not only quilting secrets and supplies that are shared among a circle of friends around the quilting frame: Celebrations, sorrows, and a little good-old-fashioned gossip all make their way into the quilting bee. And as the quilt top, batting, and backing are sewn together —three layers strong—so is the bond of the women strengthened with each carefully made stitch.

BUILDING BLOCKS
ABOVE: *This 1928 quilt booklet featured over five hundred quilt blocks. It served as a catalog from which an eager quilter could order a pattern for any block in the book, a color chart, and a sheet of detailed instructions for a mere fifteen cents.*

"WEDNESDAY KEEPS US IN STITCHES"
LEFT: *A group of women gather for their weekly quilting circle in this charming painting by Sandi Wickersham. Laughter, secrets, and a thoughtfully prepared afternoon snack are all shared as they sit and sew. (Artwork © Sandi Wickersham)*

Patchwork Quilt—Wedding Ring Design

Serving Coca-Cola Serves Hospitality

When willing fingers begin to lag, the smart hostess knows

that this is her moment. Out comes the

Coca-Cola, ice-cold—a welcome invitation

to "Refresh—add zest to the hour."

DRINK *Coca-Cola* IN BOTTLES

Coca-Cola

"Coke"

Ask for it either way ... both trade-marks mean the same thing.

The Persian Pickle Club

By Sandra Dallas

Author Sandra Dallas first began quilting thirty-five years ago and is now an avid collector of antique quilts. "I was brought up to sew," she says. "If you wanted to wear clothes, you made them." Dallas, who has written nine nonfiction books and four well-loved novels, including *Buster Midnight's Café* and *Alice's Tulips*, is a master crafter of quirky hometown characters. She currently resides in Denver, Colorado, where she serves on the board of the Rocky Mountain Quilt Museum.

In *The Persian Pickle Club*, Dallas pieces together the story of a local quilting circle in Depression-era Harveyville, Kansas. The club, named for a richly colored Victorian "Persian Pickle" or paisley fabric, is a crazy quilt of personalities. There is the strict but good-hearted Septima Judd; the sour and mean-spirited Agnes T. Ritter; the quiet and sugar-sweet Ella Crook; and our narrator, Queenie Bean, to name a few. When a city girl moves to rural Harveyville and joins the eclectic bunch, the group's long-time friendships are tested.

■ ■ ■

The first time she saw the members of the Persian Pickle Club, Rita told me after I got to know her, she thought we looked just like a bunch of setting hens. She'd learned all about setting hens that very morning after she'd gone out to the henhouse to gather eggs. Rita's luck must have been under a bucket, because Agnes T. Ritter saw her checking the roosters, and in that nasty way Agnes T. Ritter has, she told Rita just why she wasn't going to find eggs under a rooster. Then she told Rita to leave the broody hens alone unless she wanted scrambled chicks for breakfast.

How would anybody expect Rita to know about hens and roosters when she'd never lived in the country before? Like most town folks, Rita never cared where eggs came from, and after she found out, why, then she didn't care if she ever ate one again. Rita was a big city girl from Denver who had more important things to study in college than chickens, like learning how to become a famous writer. I'd never known a woman who wanted to be anything more than a farmwife.

Rita was right about us looking like a coop full of biddies. We sat there at Ada June's dining room table, clucking as Rita walked in. Then our eyes bugged out, making us look dumb enough to knit with wet spaghetti. I stopped sewing, with my hand in the air, and held it there so long that Mrs. Judd told me, "Put down your needle, Queenie Bean, and don't stare."

Well, I can tell you, I wasn't the only one staring! Even Mrs. Judd was peering with watery eyes through her little gold-rimmed glasses. How

After we quilted it, Mrs. Ritter kept the Nine-Patch in the kitchen, over the rocker, and whenever I looked at it, I searched first for the yellow zigzags I gave Rita that day, then for the pansy.

Time always went fast at the Persian Pickle Club, but that day it just flew. Even Mrs. Judd, who usually gave the high sign when it was time to go home, forgot to keep track of the hour. Not until we heard the parlor clock chime did we realize that we'd gone an hour past our time.

"Oh, dear, it's five!" Forest Ann said, as upset as if she'd looked out and seen a dust storm boiling up over the house. Ada June and I exchanged glances, and Nettie shot out an angry look, but whether it was to show her disapproval to Forest Ann or to warn the rest of us to keep our mouths shut, I couldn't tell. None of us would have breathed a word of criticism, anyway. If Forest Ann let that man stop by her house every night at five o'clock, it was her business, not ours, even if he was married.

"Sometimes I wish I didn't have a man to feed each and every evening. It'd be nice to go home to the radio and my sewing," Opalina said. She wanted to let Forest Ann know she thought being a widow wasn't always such a bad thing. I didn't look at Forest Ann, however. I looked at Ella, who didn't have a husband, either. She didn't have even a radio to keep her company. In fact, the old Crook place had no electricity, but Ella didn't mind. She sewed in the evenings by kerosene lamp—or even candlelight sometimes, because it was like having stars inside her house, she said.

Mrs. Judd looked at Ella, too. "Come along, sweetheart. You can stay to supper with me. You're better company than Prosper. He can't talk about anything but the crops drying up." The rest of us sighed, because that's all any of our husbands talked about. Mrs. Judd tucked the sugar-sack square of cloth with the butterfly she been embroidering on it into her sewing basket and stood up. "What do you say we make us a big dish of popped corn for dessert, Ella, even if it is the middle of summer? I haven't had popped corn for the longest time."

"Oh, my favorite!" Ella said.

Outside, Rita passed her hand around again for us to shake, and Ella couldn't resist touching the hem of Rita's pretty dress. "It's just like milkweed silk," she murmured.

Mrs. Judd told Rita, "You have any sewing you want done, you come see Ella here. She sews better than anybody in a hundred miles." Then she added, "She's a worker." We all nodded, because that was the biggest compliment you could give a Kansas woman. You didn't say she was smart or pretty. You said she was a worker. And Ella was a worker. In her embroidered white dress, with wisps of hair curling around her thin face, Ella resembled the girl on the Whitman's candy box, but she was a regular farmwife who chopped wood and slaughtered pigs. She was stronger than she looked—and older. She was as old as Mrs. Judd, which was more than sixty.

"Oh, I would, but I'm going learn to sew myself," Rita said, and blushed. What she meant was that she was broke like the rest of Kansas.

"You do that." Mrs. Judd opened the driver's door of the yellow Packard, and Ella scooted in across the leather seat. The old touring car sagged as Mrs. Judd stepped on the running board. I noticed she'd rolled her stockings down around her ankles when it got hot during quilting and had forgotten to roll them back up. Her legs above the rolls were angled from rickets and as white as birch sticks. Mrs. Judd sank into the seat beside Ella and started the motor, and we watched as the Packard lumbered out onto the road. Sometimes it didn't make it, and then Mrs. Judd had to tinker with the motor.

"I always think of Mutt and Jeff when I see Ella and Mrs. Judd together," Ada June whispered.

"Or Laurel and Hardy," I said.

"Or Edgar Bergen and Charlie McCarthy?" Rita chimed in. The three of us laughed about that all the way over to my car. I drove a Studebaker Commander that Grover's father had bought back when farming paid enough to live on. As I opened the door, I knew Rita was going to be more fun than a shoe box of kittens, and I turned around and hugged her, saying how glad I was she had moved to Harveyville.

CRAZY QUILT
Quilting circles are often made up of an odd assortment of dispositions and personalities, but the variety often leads to the best results—as evidenced by this 1890s Crazy quilt. The quilt's name did not come from the apparent disarray of its composition, however; most quilt historians believe that the Crazy quilt was named after the "crazing" or "cracked ice" effect that occurred in Japanese porcelain. (Minnesota Historical Society)

'84
B. PETTES

A Quilting Bee in Our Village

By Mary Eleanor Wilkins Freeman

THE QUILTING BEES of yesterday rival today's cocktail parties as boisterous social events. Women would arrive early at the home of the hostess to put in a full day's work of quilting. Meanwhile, the hostess would prepare a fabulous feast to be shared by the men of the neighborhood and the quilters themselves. Much eating, dancing, and laughing ensued—but more importantly, it was at the quilting bee celebration that young love often bloomed.

In this story, Mary Eleanor Wilkins Freeman skillfully relays the comedy and the high drama of love at a small town quilting bee. Freeman, a native of Massachusetts, recorded with subtle humor and irony her observations of New England society. Doing her best work in the 1880s and 1890s, Freeman is most well known for her collections *A Humble Romance and Other Stories* and *A New England Nun and Other Stories*.

"THE QUILTING BEE"
Missouri-based artist Bob Pettes describes his style as "Primitive Americana." In this exquisitely detailed acrylic painting, Pettes captures the camaraderie of the quilting bee, while the activity of the farm carries on in the background. (Artwork © Bob Pettes/ Nostalgic Impressions)

■ ■ ■

One sometimes wonders whether it will ever be possible in our village to attain absolute rest and completion with regard to quilts. One thinks after a week fairly swarming with quilting bees, "Now every housewife in the place must be well supplied; there will be no need to make more quilts for six months at least." Then, the next morning a nice little becurled girl in a clean pinafore knocks at the door and repeats demurely her well-conned lesson: "Mother sends her compliments, and would be happy to have you come to her quilting bee this afternoon."

One also wonders if quilts, like flowers, have their seasons of fuller production. On general principles it seems as if the winter might be more favorable to their gay complexities of bloom. In the winter there are longer evenings for merriment after the task of needlework is finished and the young men arrive; there are better opportunities for roasted apples, and chestnuts and flip, also for social games. It is easier, too, as well as pleasanter, to slip over the long miles between some of our farmhouses in a sleigh if it is only a lover and his lass, or a wood-sled if a party of neighbors or a whole family.

However, so many of our young women become betrothed in the spring, and wedded in the autumn, that the bees flourish in the hottest afternoons and evenings of midsummer.

For instance, Brama Lincoln White was engaged to William French, from Somerset, George Henry French's son, the first Sunday in July, and the very next week her mother, Mrs. Harrison White, sent out invitations to a quilting bee.

The heat during all that week was something to be remembered. It was so warm that only the very youngest and giddiest of the village people went to the Fourth of July picnic. Cyrus Emmett had a sunstroke out in the hayfield, and Mrs. Deacon Stockwell's mother, who was over ninety, was overcome by the heat and died. Mrs. Stockwell could not go to the quilting, because her mother was buried the day before. It was a misfortune to Mrs. White and Brama Lincoln, for Mrs. Stockwell is one of the fastest quilters who ever lived, but it was no especial deprivation to Mrs. Stockwell. Hardly any woman who was invited to that quilting was anxious to go. The bee was on Thursday, which was the hottest day of all that hot week. The earth seemed to give out heat like a stove, and the sky was like the lid of a fiery pot. The hot air steamed up in our faces from the ground and beat down on the tops of our heads from the sky. There was not a cool place anywhere. The village women arose before dawn, aired their rooms, then shut the windows, drew the curtains and closed blinds and shutters, excluding all the sunlight, but in an hour the heat penetrated.

Mrs. Harrison White's parlor faced southwest, and the blinds would have to be opened in order to have light enough; it seemed a hard ordeal to undergo. Lurinda Snell told Mrs. Wheelock that it did seem as if Brama Lincoln might have got ready to be married in better weather, after waiting as long as she had done. Brama was not very young, but Lurinda was older and had given up being married at all years ago. Mrs. Wheelock thought she was a little bitter, but she only pitied her for that. Lydia Wheelock is always pitying people for their sins and shortcomings instead of blaming them. She pacified Lurinda, and told her to wear her old muslin and carry her umbrella and her palm-leaf fan, and the wind was from the southwest, so there would be a breeze in Mrs. White's parlor even if it was sunny.

The women went early to the quilting; they were expected to be there at one o'clock, to secure a long afternoon for work. Eight were invited to quilt: Lurinda and Mrs. Wheelock, the young widow, Lottie Green, and five other women, some of them quite young, but master hands at such work.

Brama and her mother were not going to quilt; they had the supper to prepare. Brama's intended husband was coming over from Somerset to supper, and a number of men from our village were invited.

A few minutes before one o'clock the quilters went down the street, with their umbrellas bobbing over their heads. Mrs. Harrison White lives on the South Side in the great house where her husband keeps store. She opened the door when she saw her guests coming. She is a stout woman, and she wore a large plaid gingham dress, open at her creasy throat. Her hair clung in wet strings to her temples and her face was blazing. She had just come from the kitchen where she was baking cake. The whole house was sweet and spicy with the odor of it.

She ushered her guests into the parlor, where the great quilting-frame was stretched. It occupied nearly the entire room. There was just enough space for the quilters to file around and seat themselves four on a side. The sheet of patchwork was tied firmly to the pegs on the quilting-frame. The pattern was intricate, representing the rising sun, the number of pieces almost beyond belief; the calicoes comprising it were of the finest and brightest.

"Most all the pieces are new, an' I don't believe but what Mis' White cut them right off goods in the store," Lurinda Snell whispered to Mrs. Wheelock when the hostess had withdrawn and they had begun their labors.

They further agreed among themselves that Mrs. White and Brama must have secretly prepared the patchwork in view of some sudden and wholly uncertain matrimonial contingency.

"I don't believe but what this quilt has been pieced ever since Brama Lincoln was sixteen years old," whispered Lurinda Snell, so loud that all the women could hear her. Then suddenly she pounced forward and pointed with her sharp forefinger at a piece of green and white calico in the middle of the quilt. "There, I knew it," said she. "I remember that piece of calico in a square I saw Brama Lincoln piecing over to our house before Francis was married." Lurinda Snell has a wonderful memory.

"That's a good many years ago," said Lottie Green.

"Yes," whispered Lurinda Snell. When she whispers her s's always hiss so that they make one's ears ache, and she is very apt to whisper. "Used to be

QUILTS AND CONVERSATION

These ladies, pictured in Scranton, Iowa, in 1940, are making a quilt for a needy family. The noble work was speeded along by family news, humorous anecdotes, and scandalous pieces of small-town gossip. (Library of Congress)

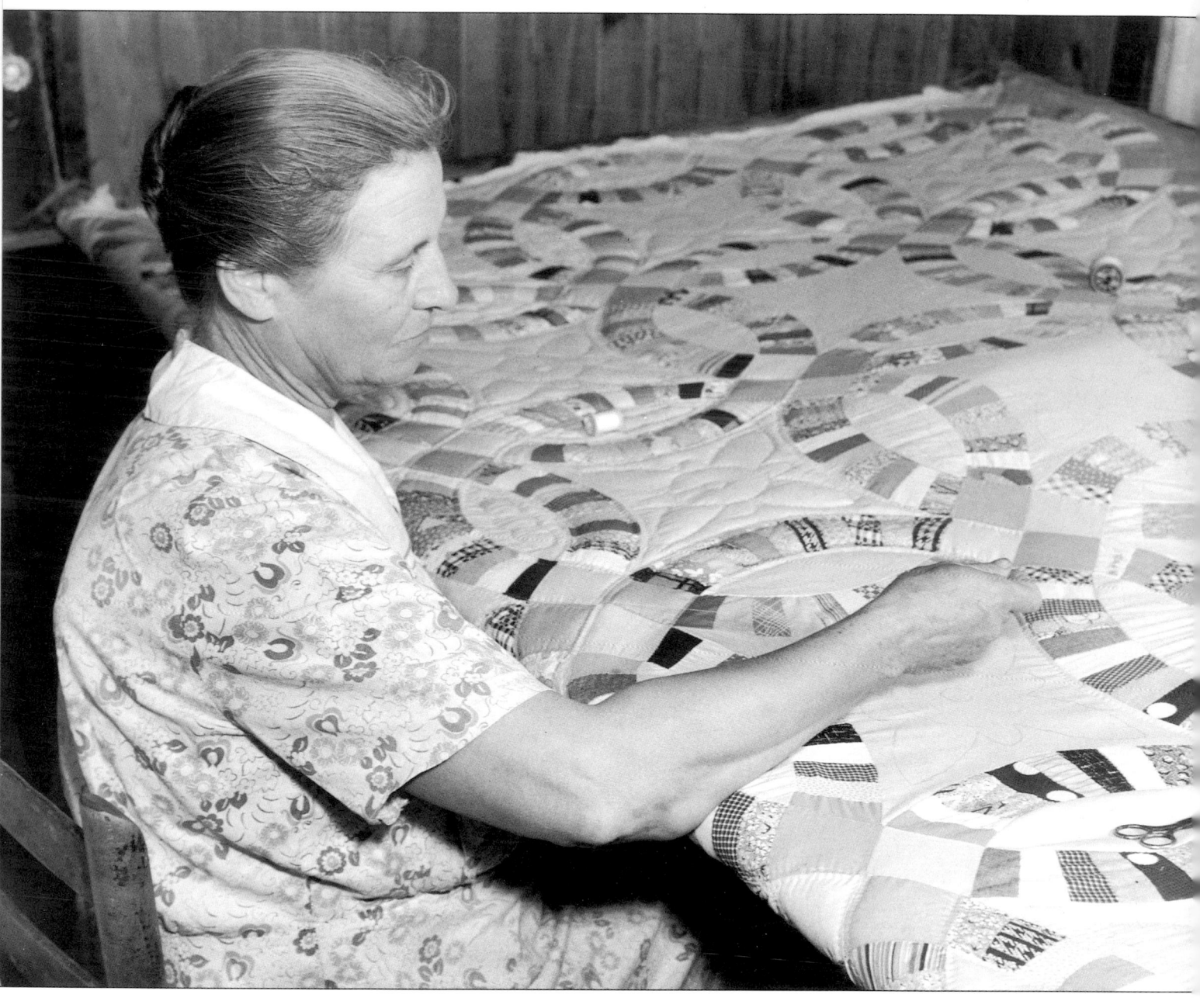

A QUILTER'S CONCENTRATION
A Louisiana quiltmaker practices her well-honed quilting stitch on a Double Wedding Ring quilt in this 1940s photograph.
(Library of Congress)

almost invariably failed to do so, and was, in consequence, kissed so many times by Mr. Downey that nearly everybody was smiling and tittering about it.

However, Lurinda Snell was exceedingly fidgety when post-office was played, and Lucius Downey had so many letters for Lottie Green, and finally she succeeded in putting a stop to the game. The post-office was in the front entry, and of course the parlor door was closed during the delivery of the letters, and Lurinda objected to that. She said the room was so warm with the entry door shut that she began to feel a buzzing in her head, which was always dangerous in her family. Her grandfather had been overheated, been seized with a buzzing in his head, and immediately dropped dead, and so had her father. When she said that, people looked anxiously at Lurinda; her face was flushed, and the post-office was given up and the entry door opened.

Next Lottie Green was called upon to sing, as she always is in company, she has such a sweet voice. She stood up in the middle of the floor, and sang "Annie Laurie" without any accompaniment, because the Slocum boy, who is not an expert musician, did not know how to play that tune, but Lurinda was taken with hiccoughs. Nobody doubted that she really had hiccoughs, but it was considered justly that she might have smothered them in her handkerchief, or at least have left the room, instead of spoiling Lottie Green's beautiful song, which she did completely. If the Slocum boy could have played the tune on his fiddle it would not have been so disastrous, but "Annie Laurie" with no accompaniment but that of hiccoughs was a failure. Brama Lincoln tiptoed out into the kitchen, and got some water for Lurinda to take nine swallows without stopping, but it did not cure her. Lurinda hiccoughed until the song was finished.

The Slocum boy tuned his fiddle then and the dancing began, but it was not a success—partly because of Lurinda and partly because of the heat. Lurinda would not dance after the first; she said her head buzzed again, but people thought—it may have been unjustly—

that she was hurt because Lucius Downey had not invited her to dance. That spoiled the set, but aside from that the room was growing insufferably warm. The windows were all wide open, but the night air came in like puffs of dark, hot steam, and swarms of mosquitoes and moths with it. The dancers were all brushing away mosquitoes and wiping their foreheads. Their faces were blazing with the heat, and even the pretty girls had a wilted and stringy look from their hair out of curl and their limp muslins.

When Lurinda refused to dance Brama Lincoln at once said that she thought it would be much pleasanter out-of-doors, and took William French by the arm and led the way. The rest of the quilting bee was held in Harrison White's front yard. The folks sat there until quite late, telling stories and singing hymns and songs. Lottie Green would not sing alone; she said it would make her too conspicuous. The front yard is next to the store, and there was a row of men on the piazza settee, besides others coming and going. The yard was light from the store windows. Brama Lincoln and William French sat as far back in the shadow as they could.

Mr. Lucius Downey sat on the door-step, out of the dampness; he considers himself delicate. Lottie Green sat on one side of him and Lurinda Snell on the other.

There was much covert curiosity as to which of the two he would escort home. Some thought he would choose Lottie, some Lurinda. The problem was solved in a most unexpected manner.

Lottie Green lives nearly a mile out of his way, in one direction, Lurinda half a mile in another. When the quilting bee disbanded, Lottie, after lingering and looking back with sweetly-pleading eyes from under her pretty white rigolette, went down the road with Lydia Wheelock's husband; Lurinda slipped forlornly up the road in the wake of a fond young couple, keeping close behind them for protection against the dangers of the night, and Mr. Lucius Downey went home by himself.

From The Minister's Wooing, 1859

By Harriet Beecher Stowe

Harriet Beecher Stowe is best known for her novel Uncle Tom's Cabin. *Here, she writes about the significant role the quilting bee plays in the lives of a newly engaged couple—even if the "ignorant and incapable sex which could not quilt" could only participate in the evening activities.*

The quilting was in those days considered the most solemn and important recognition of a betrothal. And for the benefit of those not to the manner born, a little preliminary instruction may be necessary.

The good wives of New England, impressed with that thrifty orthodoxy of economy which forbids to waste the merest trifle, had a habit of saving every scrap clipped out in the fashioning of household garments, and these they cut into fanciful patterns and constructed of them rainbow shapes and quaint traceries, the arrangement of which became one of their few fine arts. Many a maiden, as she sorted and arranged fluttering bits of green, yellow, red, and blue, felt rising in her breast a passion for somewhat vague and unknown, which came out at length in a new pattern of patchwork. Collections of these tiny fragments were always ready to fill an hour when there was nothing else to do; and as the maiden chattered with her beau, her busy flying needle stitched together those pretty bits, which, little in themselves, were destined, by gradual unions and accretions, to bring about at last substantial beauty, warmth, and comfort,—emblems thus of that household life which is to be brought to stability and beauty by reverent economy in husbanding and tact in arranging the little useful and agreeable morsels of daily existence.

When a wedding was forthcoming, there was a solemn review of the stores of beauty and utility thus provided, and the patchwork-spread best worthy of such distinction was chosen for the quilting. Thereto, duly summoned, trooped all intimate female friends of the bride, old and young; and the quilt being spread on a frame, and wadded with cotton, each vied with the others in the delicacy of the quilting she could put upon it. For the quilting also was a fine art, and had its delicacies and nice points,— which grave elderly matrons discussed with judicious care. The quilting generally began at an early hour, in the afternoon, and ended at dark with a great supper and general jubilee, at which that ignorant and incapable sex which could not quilt was allowed to appear and put in claims for consideration of another nature.

"ANNUAL QUILT SALE"

Quilting has bound communities together in many ways. The act of quilting itself connects the women who spend hours around the quilting frame; the feast and revelry following the quilting bee gathers good friends together; quilt sales and shows bring out townsfolk to admire the handiwork of their neighbors. Artist Sheila Lee, who works out of Longford Studio in Breezy Point, Minnesota, has captured the community of the quilt in this action-filled painting. (Artwork © Sheila Lee)

© Sandi Wickersham Resnick

Chapter 5

A Patchwork of Meaning & Memory

"Yes, there is the PATCHWORK QUILT! *looking to the uninterested observer like a miscellaneous collection of odd bits and ends of calico, but to me it is a precious reliquary of past treasures; a storehouse of valuables, almost destitute of intrinsic worth; a herbarium of withered flowers; a bound volume of hieroglyphics, each of which is a key to some painful or pleasant remembrance. . . ."*
—Annette (pseud.), "The Patchwork Quilt," 1845

uilts are more than just blankets to curl up in and keep us warm on cold winter nights. They also warm our souls, serving as diaries, scrapbooks, and family albums. The quilt is a tangible way to record a life's history—one square of fabric may have been cut from your favorite childhood outfit, another from the blouse you remember your mother looking so pretty in, yet another from your grandmother's wedding dress. You can follow the fabric map of the quilt to revisit the memories of generations upon generations.

The stories and recollections in this chapter patch together the philosophy that these memories are what constitute the true meaning of the quilt.

PASSING IT ON
ABOVE: *Quilts books were an excellent way for a quilter to add a new pattern to her collection—modern designs as well as tried-and-true favorites were often printed between the covers. The 1942 booklet pictured here holds such favorites as Birds in the Air, Rose of Sharon, and Roman Stripe.*

QUILT DOCTOR
LEFT: *The neighborhood horse veterinarian has arrived to pay a house call in Sandi Wickersham's painting "A Visit from Dr. Snafflebit." The quilts on the line may be in more need of a doctor, however, as two unruly goats have discovered the chewable nature of their edges. (Artwork © Sandi Wickersham)*

Everyday Use

By Alice Walker

ALICE WALKER IS the Pulitzer Prize-winning author of *The Color Purple*, as well as *The Temple of My Familiar*, *Possessing the Secret of Joy*, *By the Light of My Father's Smile*, and others. Walker, the youngest of eight children, grew up in Georgia as the daughter of poor sharecroppers. She went on to attend Spellman College in Atlanta and Sarah Lawrence in New York City before embarking on her career as a writer and civil-rights activist.

Her short story "Everyday Use" explores the dynamics between a mother and her two daughters—Maggie, who has remained with her mother on the family homestead, and Dee, who has gone to college and has rediscovered her African heritage. The daughters view the family quilt in different ways, and their mother must decide who best understands its significance and is most deserving of the precious heirloom, made by the hands of another generation.

"SOMETHING OLD, SOMETHING NEW"
A Double Wedding Ring quilt is draped over an Adirondack chair in this peaceful watercolor by Adele Earnshaw. Although the beautiful bridal quilt has been stitched for a special occasion, the quiltmaker has obviously not forgotten that above all else, a quilt is functional. (Artwork © Adele Earnshaw/Hadley Licensing)

■ ■ ■

I will wait for her in the yard that Maggie and I made so clean and wavy yesterday afternoon. A yard like this is more comfortable than most people know. It is not just a yard. It is like an extended living room. When the hard clay is swept clean as a floor and the fine sand around the edges lined with tiny, irregular grooves, anyone can come and sit and look up into the elm tree and wait for the breezes that never come inside the house.

Maggie will be nervous until after her sister goes: she will stand hopelessly in corners, homely and ashamed of the burn scars down her arms and legs, eyeing her sister with a mixture of envy and awe. She thinks her sister has held life always in the palm of one hand, that "no" is a word the world never learned to say to her.

You've no doubt seen those TV shows where the child who has "made it" is confronted, as a surprise, by her own mother and father, tottering in weakly from backstage. (A pleasant surprise, of course: What would they do if parent and child came on the show only to curse out and insult each other?) On TV mother and child embrace and smile into each other's faces. Sometimes the mother and father weep, the child wraps them in her arms and leans across the table to tell how she would not have made it without their help. I have seen these programs.

Sometimes I dream a dream in which Dee and I are suddenly brought together on a TV program of this sort. Out of a dark and soft-seated limousine I am ushered into a bright room filled with many people. There I meet a smiling, gray, sporty man like Johnny Carson who shakes my

BARN RAISING
Classic variations on the Log Cabin quilt include the Pineapple, Straight Furrows, Light and Dark, Courthouse Steps, and Windmill Blades arrangements. The Barn Raising variation, as illustrated by this 1860 quilt from the collection of Kitty Clark Cole, is one of the most popular and striking Log Cabin variations. (Photograph © Keith Baum/BaumsAway!)

make-believe, burned us with a lot of knowledge we didn't necessarily need to know. Pressed us to her with the serious way she read, to shove us away at just the moment, like dimwits, we seemed about to understand.

Dee wanted nice things. A yellow organdy dress to wear to her graduation from high school; black pumps to match a green suit she'd made from an old suit somebody gave me. She was determined to stare down any disaster in her efforts. Her eyelids would not flicker for minutes at a time. Often I fought off the temptation to shake her. At sixteen she had a style of her own: and knew what style was.

I never had an education myself. After second grade the school was closed down. Don't ask my why: in 1927 colored asked fewer questions than they do now. Sometimes Maggie reads to me. She stumbles along good-naturedly but can't see well. She knows she is not bright. Like good looks and money, quickness passes her by. She will marry John Thomas (who has mossy teeth in an earnest face) and then I'll be free to sit here and I guess just sing church songs to myself. Although I never was a good singer. Never could carry a tune. I was always better at a man's job. I used to love to milk till I was hooked in the side in '49. Cows are soothing and slow and don't bother you, unless you try to milk them the wrong way.

I have deliberately turned my back on the house. It is three rooms, just like the one that burned, except the roof is tin; they don't make shingle roofs any more. There are no real windows, just some holes cut in the sides, like the portholes in a ship, but not round and not square, with rawhide holding the shutters up on the outside. This house is in a pasture, too, like the other one. No doubt when Dee sees it she will want to tear it down. She wrote me once that no matter where we "choose" to live, she will manage to come see us. But she will never bring her friends. Maggie and I thought about this and Maggie asked me, "Mama, when did Dee ever *have* any friends?"

She had a few. Furtive boys in pink shirts hanging about on washday after school. Nervous girls who never laughed. Impressed with her they worshipped the well-turned phrase, the cute shape, the scalding humor that erupted like bubbles in lye. She read to them.

When she was courting Jimmy T she didn't have much time to pay to us, but turned all her faultfinding power on him. He *flew* to marry a cheap city girl from

SISTER'S CHOICE
The simplicity of a blue and white color scheme heightens the perfection of a well-pieced quilt. This example comes from Sylvia Petersheim Quilts & Crafts of Bird-in-Hand, Pennsylvania. (Photograph © Keith Baum/BaumsAway!)

A QUILT BY ANY OTHER NAME
It was common for the same quilt pattern to have different names in different parts of North America. This quilt block was known by several names, including Bear's Paw, Duck's Foot in the Mud, and Hand of Friendship. Sina R. Phillips of Muskegon, Michigan, knows the pattern, featured on her 1983 quilt, as Crow Foot in the Mud. (Courtesy of Michigan State University Museum)

he told me to just call him Hakim-a-barber. I wanted to ask him was he a barber, but I didn't really think he was, so I didn't ask.

"You must belong to those beef-cattle peoples down the road," I said. They said "Asalamalakim" when they met you, too, but they didn't shake hands. Always too busy: feeding the cattle, fixing the fences, putting up salt-lick shelters, throwing down hay. When the white folks poisoned some of the herd the men stayed up all night with rifles in their hands. I walked a mile and a half just to see the sight.

Hakim-a-barber said, "I accept some of their doctrines, but farming and raising cattle is not my style." (They didn't tell me, and I didn't ask, whether Wangero (Dee) had really gone and married him.)

We sat down to eat and right away he said he didn't eat collards and pork was unclean. Wangero, though, went on through the chitlins and corn bread, the greens and everything else. She talked a blue streak over the sweet potatoes. Everything delighted her. Even the fact that we still used the benches her daddy made for the table when we couldn't afford to buy chairs.

"Oh, Mama!" she cried. Then turned to Hakim-a-barber. "I never knew how lovely these benches are. You can feel the rump prints," she said, running her hands underneath her and along the bench. Then she gave a sigh and her hand closed over Grandma Dee's butter dish. "That's it!" she said. "I knew there was something I wanted to ask you if I could have." She jumped up from the table and went over in the corner where the churn stood, the milk in it clabber by now. She looked at the churn and looked at it.

"This churn top is what I need," she said. "Didn't Uncle Buddy whittle it out of a tree you all used to have?"

"Yes," I said.

"Un huh," she said happily. "And I want the dasher, too."

"Uncle Buddy whittle that, too?" asked the barber.

Dee (Wangero) looked up at me.

"Aunt Dee's first husband whittled the dash," said Maggie so low you almost couldn't hear her. "His name was Henry, but they called him Stash."

"Maggie's brain is like an elephant's," Wangero said, laughing. "I can use the churn top as a center-piece for the alcove table," she said, sliding a plate over the churn, "and I'll think of something artistic to do with the dasher."

When she finished wrapping the dasher the handle stuck out. I took it for a moment in my hands. You didn't even have to look close to see where hands pushing the dasher up and down to make butter had left a kind of sink in the wood. In fact, there were a lot of small sinks; you could see where thumbs and fingers had sunk into the wood. It was beautiful light yellow wood, from a tree that grew in the yard where Big Dee and Stash had lived.

After dinner Dee (Wangero) went to the trunk at the foot of my bed and started rifling through it. Maggie hung back in the kitchen over the dishpan. Out came Wangero with two quilts. They had been pieced by Grandma Dee and then Big Dee and me had hung them on the quilt frames on the front porch and quilted them. One was in the Lone Star pattern. The other was Walk Around the Mountain. In both of them were scraps of dresses Grandma Dee had worn fifty and more years ago. Bits and pieces of Grandpa Jarrell's Paisley shirts. And one teeny faded blue piece, about the size of a penny matchbox, that was from Great Grandpa Ezra's uniform that he wore in the Civil War.

"Mama," Wangero said sweet as a bird. "Can I have these old quilts?"

I heard something fall in the kitchen, and a minute later the kitchen door slammed.

"Why don't you take one or two of the others?" I asked. "These old things was just done by me and Big Dee from some tops your grandma pieced before she died."

"No," said Wangero. "I don't want those. They are stitched around the borders by machine."

"That'll make them last better," I said.

"That's not the point," said Wangero. "These are all pieces of dresses Grandma used to wear. She did all this stitching by hand. Imagine!" She held the quilts securely in her arms, stroking them.

"Some of the pieces, like those lavender ones, come from old clothes her mother handed down to her," I said, moving up to touch the quilts. Dee (Wangero) moved back just enough so that I couldn't reach the quilts. They already belonged to her.

"Imagine!" she breathed again, clutching them closely to her bosom.

"The truth is," I said, "I promised to give them quilts to Maggie, for when she marries John Thomas."

She gasped like a bee had stung her.

"Maggie can't appreciate these quilts!" she said. "She'd probably be backward enough to put them to everyday use."

"I reckon she would," I said. "God knows I been saving 'em for long enough with nobody using 'em. I hope she will!" I didn't want to bring up how I had offered Dee (Wangero) a quilt when she went away to college. Then she had told they were old-fashioned, out of style.

"But they're *priceless!*" she was saying now, furiously; for she has a temper. "Maggie would put them on the bed and in five years they'd be in rags. Less than that!"

"She can always make some more," I said. "Maggie knows how to quilt."

Dee (Wangero) looked at me with hatred. "You just will not understand. The point is these quilts, *these* quilts!"

"Well," I said, stumped. "What would *you* do with them?"

"Hang them," she said. As if that was the only thing you *could* do with quilts.

Maggie by now was standing in the door. I could almost hear the sound her feet made as they scraped over each other.

"She can have them, Mama," she said, like somebody used to never winning anything, or having anything reserved for her. "I can 'member Grandma Dee without the quilts."

I looked at her hard. She had filled her bottom lip with checkerberry snuff and gave her face a kind of dopey, hangdog look. It was Grandma Dee and Big Dee who taught her how to quilt herself. She stood there with her scarred hands hidden in the folds of her skirt. She looked at her sister with something like fear but she wasn't mad at her. This was Maggie's portion. This was the way she knew God to work.

When I looked at her like that something hit me in the top of my head and ran down to the soles of my feet. Just like when I'm in church and the spirit of God touches me and I get happy and shout. I did something I never done before: hugged Maggie to me, then dragged her on into the room, snatched the quilts out of Miss Wangero's hands and dumped them into Maggie's lap. Maggie just sat there on my bed with her mouth open.

"Take one or two of the others," I said to Dee.

But she turned without a word and went out to Hakim-a-barber.

"You just don't understand," she said, as Maggie and I came out to the car.

"What don't I understand?" I wanted to know.

"Your heritage," she said. And then she turned to Maggie, kissed her, and said, "You ought to try to make something of yourself, too, Maggie. It's really a new day for us. But from the way you and Mama still live you'd never know it."

She put on some sunglasses that hid everything above the tip of her nose and chin.

Maggie smiled; maybe at the sunglasses. But a real smile, not scared. After we watched the car dust settle I asked Maggie to bring me a dip of snuff. And then the two of us sat there just enjoying, until it was time to go in the house and go to bed.

Mosaic

This hand-pieced and -quilted Mosaic Checkerboard quilt was made circa 1900. The small cotton squares that compose this quilt promise that even the littlest scrap of fabric could be utilized in its design. (Courtesy of Washington County MN Historical Society, photograph by Tomy O'Brien)

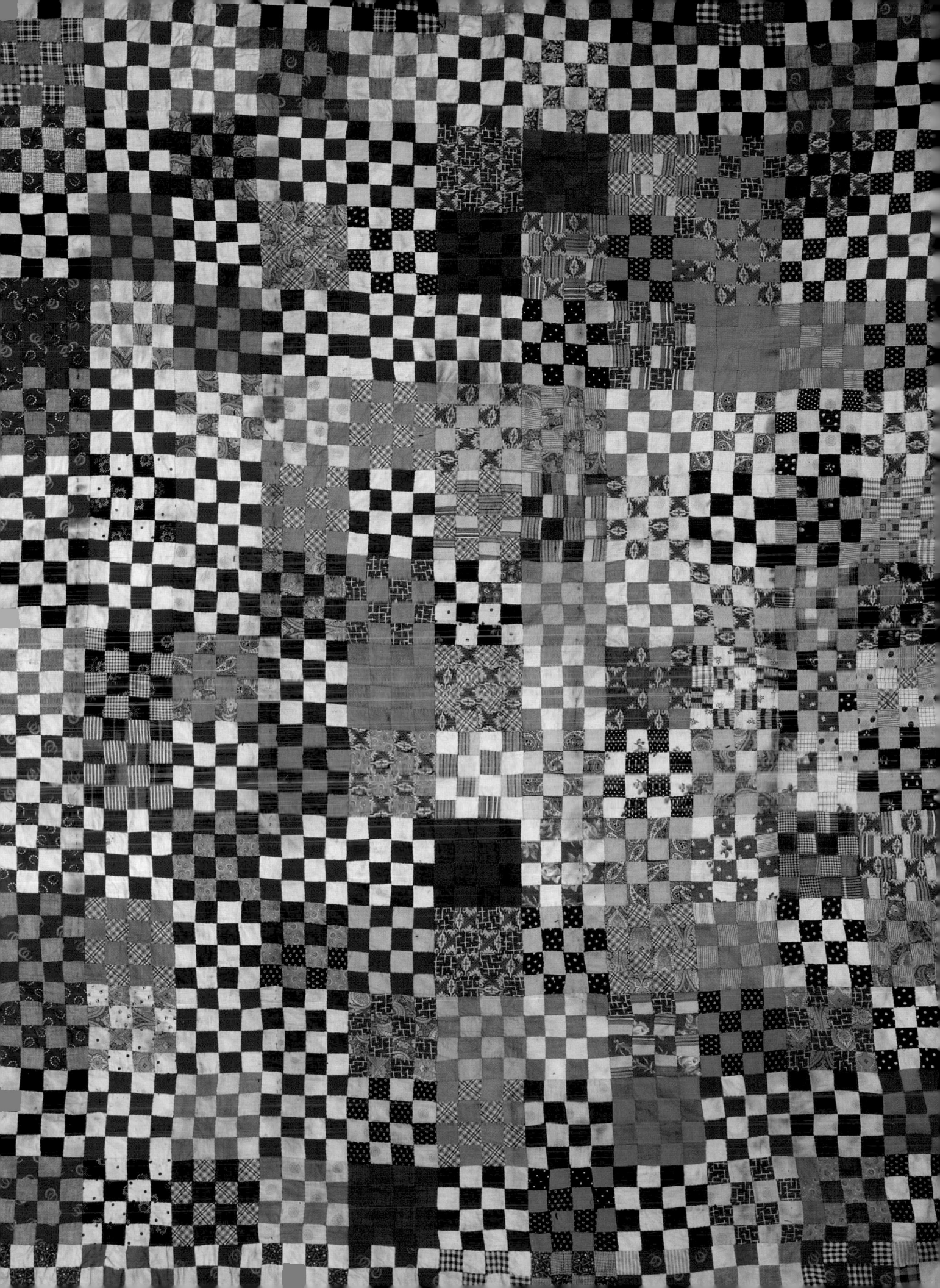

Aunt Jane's Album

By *Eliza Calvert Hall*

ELIZA CALVERT HALL, the pen name of Eliza Calvert Obenchain, grew up in Bowling Green, Kentucky. She became an author and suffragist, taking time off from her efforts to ensure a woman's right to vote to write her timeless stories, which focused on the women of her native state at the turn of the twentieth century.

Aunt Jane of Kentucky, from which this excerpt is taken, was first published in 1907. In it, Hall introduces a wise, eighty-year-old spinster named Aunt Jane who we share an afternoon with as she studies the kaleidoscope of quilts on her clothesline and remembers the story behind each one.

■ ■ ■

"GRANDMA'S ATTIC"
A trunk full of treasures are packed away in this delightful painting by Doug Knutson. As sunlight streams through the window, the well-used quilt and sewing machine seem to patiently wait for someone to come and rediscover them. (Artwork © Doug Knutson/ Apple Creek Publishing)

They were a bizarre mass of color on the sweet spring landscape, those patchwork quilts, swaying in a long line under the elms and maples. The old orchard made a blossoming background for them, and farther off on the horizon rose the beauty of fresh verdure and purple mist on those low hills, or "knobs," that are to the heart of the Kentuckian as the Alps to the Swiss or the sea to the sailor.

I opened the gate softly and paused for a moment between the blossoming lilacs that grew on each side the path. The fragrance of the white and the purple blooms was like a resurrection-call over the graves of many a dead spring; and as I stood, shaken with thoughts as the flowers are with the winds, Aunt Jane came around from the back of the house, her black silk cape fluttering from her shoulders, and a calico sunbonnet hiding her features in its cavernous depth. She walked briskly to the clothes-line and began patting and smoothing the quilts where the breeze had disarranged them.

"Aunt Jane," I called out, "are you having a fair all by yourself?"

She turned quickly pushing back the sunbonnet from her eyes.

"Why, child," she said, with a happy laugh, "you come pretty nigh skeerin' me. No, I ain't havin' any fair; I'm jest givin' my quilts their spring airin'. Twice a year I put 'em out in the sun and wind; and this mornin' the air smelt so sweet, I thought it was a good chance to freshen 'em up for the summer. It's about time to take 'em in now."

She began to fold the quilts and lay them over her arm, and I did the same. Back and forth we went from the clothes-line to the house, and from the house to the clothes-line, until the quilts were safely housed from the coming dewfall and piled on every available chair in the front room. I looked at them in sheer amazement. There seemed to be every pattern that the ingenuity of woman could devise and the industry of woman put together,—"four-patches," "nine-patches," "log-cabins," "wild-goose chases," "rising suns," hexagons, diamonds, and only Aunt Jane knows what else. As for color, a Sandwich Islander would have danced with joy at the sight of those reds, purples, yellows, and greens.

"Did you really make all these quilts, Aunt Jane?" I asked wonderingly.

Aunt Jane's eyes sparkled with pride.

"Every stitch of 'em, child," she said, "except the quiltin'. The neighbors used to come in and help some with that. I've heard folks say that piecin' quilts was nothin' but a waste o' time, but that ain't always so. They used to say that Sarah Jane Mitchell would set down right after breakfast and piece till it was time to git dinner, and then set and piece till she had to git supper, and then piece by candle-light till she fell asleep in her cheer.

"I ricollect goin' over there one day, and Sarah Jane was gittin' dinner in a big hurry, for Sam had to go to town with some cattle, and there was a big basket o' quilt pieces in the middle o' the kitchen floor,

Quilts often look their best when accompanied by warm summer sunshine and a gentle breeze. This Spider Web antique quilt of unknown origin was re-quilted by the 'Snobelt Quilters and assembled by Vita Challone of New York, and is now ready for another generation to enjoy. (Photograph © Dianne Dietrich Leis)

and the house lookin' like a pigpen, and the children runnin' around half naked. And Sam he laughed, and says he, 'Aunt Jane, if we could wear quilts and eat quilts we'd be the richest people in the country.' Sam was the best-natured man that ever was, or he couldn't 'a' put up with Sarah Jane's shiftless ways. Hannah Crawford said she sent Sarah Jane a bundle o' caliker once by Sam, and Sam always declared he lost it. But Uncle Jim Matthews said he was ridin' along the road jest behind Sam, and he saw Sam throw it into the creek jest as he got on the bridge. I never blamed Sam a bit if he did.

"But there never was any time wasted on my quilts, child. I can look at every one of 'em with a clear conscience. I did my work faithful; and then, when I might 'a' set and held my hands, I'd make a block or two o' patchwork, and before long I'd have enough to put together in a quilt. I went to piecin' as soon as I was

MUSSLEMAN STAR

Great care must be taken with an antique quilt to ensure that it will be preserved for future generations. It is likely that the old quilts that survive today were the "best" quilts of their original makers and were used infrequently. This rosy-hued quilt from the collection of Kitty Clark Cole has been passed down through the years since it was made in 1885. (Photograph © Keith Baum/BaumsAway!)

"Pieced and Patched"

This article from a vintage Modern Priscilla *magazine revives a collection of favorite old quilt blocks. The designs included are Rose in a Ring, Sunrise, The Fan, Hickory Leaf, Dove at the Window, Mill Wheel, and Gentleman's Fancy, which the description points out is "the lady's too, unless we are much mistaken."*

old enough to hold a needle and a piece o' cloth, and one o' the first things I can remember was settin' on the back door-step sewin' my quilt pieces, and mother praisin' my stitches. Nowadays folks don't have to sew unless they want to, but when I was a child there warn't any sewin'-machines, and it was about as needful for folks to know how to sew as it was for 'em to know how to eat; and every child that was well raised could hem and run and backstitch and gether and overhand by the time she was nine years old. Why, I'd pieced four quilts by the time I was nineteen years old, and when we and Abram set up housekeepin' I had bed-clothes enough for three beds.

"I've had a heap o' comfort all my life makin' quilts, and now in my old age I wouldn't take a fortune for 'em. Set down here, child, where you can see out o' the winder and smell the lilacs, and we'll look at 'em all. You see, some folks has albums to put folks' pictures in to remember 'em by, and some folks has a book and writes down the things that happen every day so they won't forgit 'em; but, honey, these quilts is my albums and my di'ries, and whenever the weather's bad and I can't git out to see folks, I jest spread out my quilts and look at 'em and study over 'em, and it's jest like goin' back fifty or sixty years and livin' my life over agin."

Log Cabin House
House quilts, including Schoolhouse and Log Cabin variations, were old favorites in the quilting community, but experienced an increased popularity in the 1920s and 1930s. This example was made circa 1920 and comes from the collection of Kitty Clark Cole. (Photograph © Keith Baum/BaumsAway!)

The Quilters

By Patricia J. Cooper and Norma Bradley Allen

CHILDHOOD FRIENDS PATRICIA Cooper and Norma Bradley Allen collaborated in the early 1970s to record numerous first-person accounts of the female quilters who were some of the pioneering settlers of Texas and New Mexico. Remembrances both uplifting and moving were documented by Cooper and Allen, who noted that "As the quilters talked about quilts they were constantly reminded of some other parts of their lives, a story about pioneering times, an anecdote about a family member, or some technical detail of quilting. The quilts seemed to be the format in which they had condensed much of personal, family, and community history."

The Quilters brought some much-deserved attention to the art of the quilt. It won several book awards, became a supplementary college textbook, and was adapted into a musical by Molly Newman and Barbara Damashek, which was nominated for seven Tony Awards.

Patricia Cooper taught at the University of California at Berkley until her death in 1987. Norma Bradley Allen continues to write, living on an old farm in Cedar Hill, Texas. Each of the following pieces recalls the story of a different quilter who Cooper and Allen had the pleasure to interview in their efforts to preserve the meaning and memory of the American quilt.

■ ■ ■

When I was little we had dark comforts made from old overalls and wool trousers on our beds. Sometimes the neighbor women would come in and quilt with Mama. Now them quilts was always real pretty. I wanted to keep some of the pretty, bright-colored quilts but Mama would say that we could make do with what we had. Others needed them more.

My mama quilted every day until I was four and the third child was born. Then there was nowhere to put the frame up and leave it. One day a week, when the neighbors came to quilt, my brother would take the bed in Mama's room down to the kitchen and put up the frame for that day. It was quite a job, but he never minded. There was no more than four women working because there was no room for more.

I remember standing in the doorway with my thumb in my mouth watching them. Sometimes I waited and waited for the women to go home because I was hungry. But it wasn't proper for a child to ask for food when there was company in the house. Dad was always proud of Mama on quilting days. When he came inside from work he would say how busy she had been. He knew that she had a hard and lonely life; he was happy that she could enjoy quilting. When neighbor women came over for the day, he was glad she could have a day with her friends and enjoy herself. He always spoke kindly to ever' one.

They took all the pretty quilts to the Baptist Church. They was for the poor people and foreign missions. And sometimes if somebody lost their house to a fire or a twister, the women would all go with a stack of quilts and say, "These is a gift from the ladies of the First Baptist Church."

I can remember even back before I was old enough to quilt, my mother and older sisters would be quiltin' and us little ones had to keep their needles threaded. We'd be out in the yard playin' and they'd holler they needed some needles. We had a whole bunch of needles that we'd run in and thread and stick 'em on top of the quilt for them. Then when they run out of needles threaded, here they'd holler again.

There was six girls and one boy in my family. We all quilted and pieced together. I can remember Mama even saved her strings and cut them into long, thin strips for some pattern she had in mind like a Log Cabin or Windmill Blades. Then she would cut me a square piece of paper and I'd sew them strings across there in rows. They had to be the same width that I'd measure with my school ruler. I can remember it just as well.

My husband tells about the time he got sick with the measles. He was six years old. His mother set him to piecing a quilt and every other block he set in red polka-dot pattern. Said it was his measles quilt. He wouldn't like me to tell it now I know. But lots of cold nights when I'm at the quiltin' frame on one side of the fire, he pulls his big old chair up on the other side and cuts pieces for me. He's even done a bit of piecin' from time to time.

It's a sight, that big old long-legged man with his boot toes turned in to make a lap to do his piecework on.

We've got a fair long road from the highway and three loud dogs out there. They all always sound off when somebody turns up our road. And let me tell you, he can git rid of that work quicker than a gnat can bat an eye, when them dogs commence to barkin'.

Plumb tickles me.

I'm eighty-three and I've done a heap of quilts, girl. But I remember, like it was yesterday, my first quilt. Mama had one of them frames that swung down from

over the bed and there was always a quilt in it. She quilted for the public, to help pay our way. Now, we might take one out late one night when it was finished and wait till mornin' to put the next one in. But that was as long as it ever was.

Mama was a beautiful quilter. She done the best work in the county. Everybody knew it. She never let nobody else touch her quilts; and sometimes when she was through quiltin' for the day on a job that she liked a lot herself, she would pin a cloth over the top of the quilt so nobody could look at it till she was done.

I always longed to work with her and I can tell you how plain I recall the day she said, "Sarah, you come quilt with me now if you want to."

I was too short to sit in a chair and reach it, so I got my needle and thread and stood beside her. I put that needle through and pulled it back up again, then down, and my stitches were about three inches long. Papa come in about that time, he stepped back and said, "Florence, that child is flat ruinin' your quilt."

Mama said, "She's doin' no kind of a thing. She's quiltin' her first quilt."

He said, "Well, you're jest goin' to have to rip it all out tonight."

Mama smiled at me and said, "Them stitches is going to be in that quilt when it wears out."

All the time they was talkin' my stitches was gettin' shorter.

That was my first quilt. I have it still to look at sometimes.

My daddy was a Baptist preacher. I reckon you can tell that by how ornery I am. We didn't have much luxury, I can say. But I remember the funniest day one time when I was still a young girl.

Mama was goin' to help me start my quilts for my hope chest. She had got the old scrap bag out. We spread 'em all out on the bed and tried to kinda put the colors together right. But the scrap bag was really low. We sure hadn't got anything new in a long time and it seemed at that time everybody in the church was usin' all their own scraps and none had come our way.

Mama said, "Come on into town with me Saturday, and we'll just pick up a few pieces of brighter calico to spruce 'em up a bit."

Well, come Saturday, true to her word, we went to town with Papa. Soon as he tied up the team he

POSTAGE STAMP STARS
The construction of "competitive" quilts made with thousands of tiny pieces began in the late nineteenth century. A quilt with over 10,000 pieces was considered a "record-breaker" in the 1920s, and was often written up in the newspaper as a local wonder, but the number rose quickly. In 1948, Grace Snyder of North Platte, Nebraska, used 87,789 minuscule triangles in her Petit Point Flower Basket quilt. The 1880 Mennonite quilt pictured here from the collection of Kitty Clark Cole shows an equal balance of quantity of pieces and quality of craftsmanship. (Photograph © Keith Baum/BaumsAway!)

GALLERY OF FOLK ART
Sandi Wickersham celebrates several forms of folk art in her contemporary painting "Sampler of American Folk Life." Inside the cozy log cabin is a hand-painted chest, a needle-work sampler, a beautiful rug, a knitting project in progress, a stack of quilts, and a faithful reproduction of the famous folk art painting "Girl in Red Dress with Cat and Dog" by Ammi Phillips, which was originally painted in the early to mid 1830s. (Artwork © Sandi Wickersham)

©Sardi Wickersham Resnick

went over to the feed store and we went to the dry goods. We had picked three pieces of remnant blue and was just fingerin' some red calico. We was jest plannin' on enough for the middle squares from that.

Just then Papa come in behind us and I guess he saw us lookin'. He just walked right past us like he wasn't with us, right up to the clerk and said, "How much cloth is on that bolt?"

The clerk said, "Twenty yards."

Papa never looked around. He just said, "I'll take it all!"

He picked up that whole bolt of red calico and carried it to the wagon. Mama and me just laughed to beat the band. Twenty yards of red. Can you imagine?

A Baptist preacher, jest like any other man, likes that red. We had red for a long, long time.

We were living out in the country when we first married, and we just didn't have much. When the kids started coming along there was lots of quilting to be done.

For a while I pieced on the halves for people around. Some folks were doing better than us, and they would get together enough material for two quilts. I would piece both of them, and for my work I got to keep one for nothing. Then one time Mama came to see me. I told her what I was doing. She said, "You're not going to have to do that any more!" Later, after she went back home, she sent me out a great big flour sack stuffed full of scraps. It was a gift that always meant a lot to me.

Now I have some ten big scrap bags. If someone else were to see them, they would seem like a pile of junk, but I've got all my pieces sorted according to the color. Got my cottons here and my polyester's there. I've been told I have a way with matching up my colors. It comes natural to me. I keep figuring and working with my materials, and thinking about my colors a long time before it feels right. I know how my quilt is going to look before I ever start.

Different ones of my family are always appearing from one of these bags. Just when you thought you'd forgotten someone, well, like right here . . . I remem-

ber that patch. That was a dress that my grandmother wore to church. I sat beside her singing hymns, and that dress was so pretty to me then. I can just remember her in that dress now.

I belonged to this club out in Hamilton. It was just a quiltin' club. Everybody taken a covered dish and we just quilted. Whoever had the club put up a quilt, and we quilted it out. Sometime we'd quilt two a day. Some days they would be fifteen or twenty of us all over that quilt. Some of 'em didn't do too good a quiltin'. When it come my time I didn't put up no fancy quilt. I just put up one I didn't care how was quilted. Lot of 'em did the same thing. I'd put up a string quilt, or just something I didn't care who quilted on it.

I remember a girl. She was newly married. She had a baby and she joined our club. She had never quilted before and I don't reckon she'd ever seen anybody quilt. She'd belonged to our club, I don't know how long, two or three weeks or maybe a month, before she found out we was going down from the top and plump through the lining with each stitch. You know what? She was workin' on all her stitches so hard and they was just goin' through the top . . . jest quiltin' along on the top. Would you ever think there could be anybody that dumb? She was a sweet little ole girl, but she jest didn't know no better. "Well, I didn't know you was goin' all the way through," she said. Why everybody in that room jest died. I laughed and everybody did. It was funny, but I felt sorry for her, she hated it so bad.

I quilt some everyday. It just keeps me going. When I quilt I just set down here and go at it. I never liked to quilt with a group, only with my mother when I was young. She taught me to quilt and we liked it to always be right. I don't like somebody else working on my quilt. You know, maybe they didn't learn the way I did.

I sit here and quilt facin' this way most of the time. See, I put all my family pictures up there in front of me so I can look at them while I quilt. They are all around me that way.

MARINER'S COMPASS
The simply drawn compass that appeared on sea charts was likely the inspiration for this quilt design, which dates back to the eighteenth century. The "folky" version of the popular pattern pictured here comes from the collection of Kitty Clark Cole and was constructed in 1880. (Photograph © Keith Baum/BaumsAway!)

SOFT QUILTS, HARD TIMES
During the Great Depression, quilting brought a bit of much-needed color and optimism to many women. Patchwork was conducive to times of economic hardship, as many patterns could be made with scraps of fabric. A bespectacled woman of the Depression proudly displays her Dresden Plate quilt in this 1936 photograph. (Library of Congress)

I have my son up there four times. When he was small and playin', when he graduated from high school, when he was in the war, and with his grandchildren. I look at all those boys and men and think on him.

There's my daughter looking to be the same age as my aunt. They were a lot like one another, too. But, of course, my aunt had passed on before my girl was even born. It's a pleasure puttin' it all together.

There's no way in the world I could even guess how many quilts I've worked in my time. But I do know that I've supplied a lot of households with them. My husband was a minister and we were always involved in charity, either gettin' it or givin' it. So when I was younger I had a stack of quilts that was higher than your head, just inside the front door in the hall-way. I used them for gifts—Christmas, weddings, and to divide with the poor. Now all the quilts I have are for my five kids and for all the grandchildren. And now their kids are wanting quilts of their own. I just tell them that as long as they keep bringin' me scraps and likin' my quilts, I'll keep doin'.

I like to do that little half square. A body never throws a bit of scrap in the trash piecin' that one. You can use it all. And they come out real bright and pretty. I get good feelin' workin' on that one.

I do my piecing by feel. I can't hardly see nothin' no more. People don't believe I pieced those. I pieced this one after I was nearly blind and you can just turn it over and look at my stitches. They are little, let me tell you. I can thread a needle still. I just point and thread. No, really I have a little invention that I do just like a puzzle. Don't need no help for that. I pieced quilts when I was a child. It's natural for me to sew and make things. My whole family pieced, but I think I cap 'em all. That's not nice for me to say, but I was the oldest girl and learned the longest with Mama.

I want to show you this quilt. And if anybody asks you, I will sell some of these dirt cheap. I have twenty quilts here now, and I have given away about thirty. Now this one here is like a puzzle. See, it has a star and a ninepatch, and I don't know what all. I have a friend in Oklahoma that's a great hand to piece quilts, and she gave me the pattern and I brought it home

with me. It's a lot of fun to do. I can't even remember how to do it now. My stepmother pieced this quilt and I think it's real pretty. I cut the colors out for her to piece. I just love to work with quilts. They make a big old mess; you know what I mean? But I just love it. This is a string quilt. You get to use all your little pieces making one of these.

I've made several quilts for people who had the misfortune to burn out and lose all their bedding, and other things. Our club makes quilts for folks in times of trouble. I quilt in a club that sometimes quilts two quilts in one day. We go and have a covered-dish lunch and work all day.

When we was little and moved out to this terri-tory it was plenty cold in the winter, and we had to get busy right away and make quilts for the younger kids. Mama had a few worn-out things and I remember some people gave us some scraps. My grandmother lived with us most of the time and she was a good hand to quilt, and she knitted too. But quilting then was the big object, and we would quilt about eight or ten quilts a year. But you see there was so many of us, it took lots of quilts. My mother had a stack of quilts when she died, and I told my stepmother to save we children one apiece. I have one of them now. I'll get up in the closet and show it to you if you want to see it. It's high, but I don't intend to ever fall. Here's the one my mama made. It's set together in rows like slats in a fence. She called it Fence Row. They used to make lots of quilts like that.

Now my grandmother gave me this and it is older than I am. These tiny blocks all matches except in this one corner. As a little girl, I used to wonder why she didn't get some more of the right color to finish it with. I remember this patch here . . . that was the dress my grandmother had that was so pretty to me then. I can just remember her in that.

Most people don't like to quilt. They think it's too little a business, I guess. Too much work involved. I love to quilt. My husband used to say, "I just have to choke you off a quilt." He did want me to come and eat when the family did, of course. But oh, I'd rather quilt than eat when I'm hungry.

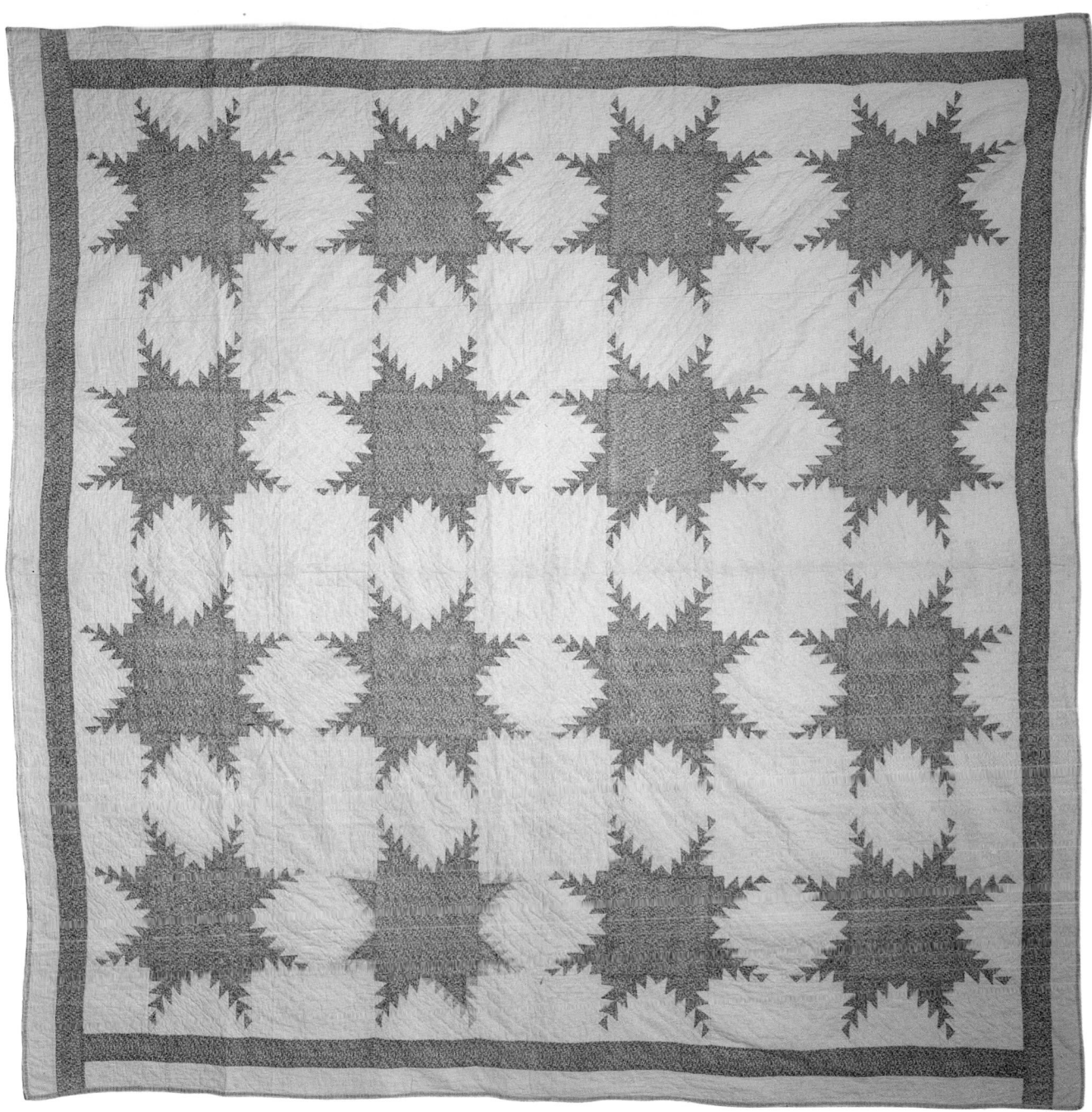

FEATHERED STARS

This design required a significant amount of skill, so it was often reserved for special quilts. "Double pink" fabric—cotton fabric that has two shades of pink on a white background—was popular in the mid to late 1800s when this quilt was made. (Courtesy of Washington County MN Historical Society, photograph by Tomy O'Brien)

QUILT OF GOOD WILL

Symbols were often incorporated into quilts to convey a special meaning. The Pineapple represents hospitality—a gesture so often shared within the quilting community. This Pineapple Log Cabin variation, circa 1865, comes from the collection of Kitty Clark Cole. (Photograph © Keith Baum/BaumsAway!)